HISTORY AND HISTORIANS

Some Essays

Davis D. Joyce
The University of Tulsa

UNIVERSITY
PRESS OF
AMERICA

For my parents

Gladys and A. A. "Bud" Joyce

iii

Acknowledgements

Several of the pieces in this book appeared previously elsewhere. I would like to thank Dorothy Mauldin for helping me publish privately an earlier pamphlet edition of "History: Definitions, Reasons, and Methods." My colleague, Thomas H. Buckley, and my graduate assistant at the time, Carl Goosen, provided helpful advice on the manuscript at that stage. "American Historian: Edward Channing, 1856-1931" appeared in the Summer, 1974, edition of Historical Musings, and is reprinted here with the permission of Dale E. Landon, who was the co-editor of the journal at that time. I also thank John S. Ezell, who directed my Ph. D. dissertation on Channing, and whose support of my work over the years has been invaluable. The reviews of books by Weinstein and Gatell, Lichtman and French, and Reinitz all appeared in The History Teacher (in November of 1973, May of 1979, and May of 1982, respectively), and are reprinted here with permission. The Canadian Journal of History kindly granted permission to reprint the review of Guberman's book from its April, 1975 issue. Stephen Kneeshaw, editor of the excellent little journal Teaching History, gave permission to use the review of the Marcus book (from the Spring, 1981, issue), as well as the article "The Past Through Tomorrow: Understanding History Through Science Fiction" (Fall, 1978), which benefitted greatly from his expert editing. W. Wayne Smith accepted my article, "Revising History with Ecology," while he was editor of the Social Studies Journal (Spring, 1978) and gave permission to reprint it here. Finally, the Red River Valley Historical Review approved the reprinting of "Before Teapot Dome: Senator Albert B. Fall and Conservation" from its Fall, 1979, issue. I also gratefully acknowledge the assistance of Ira G. Clark, who directed my M. A. thesis, from which this article developed. Thanks to one and all.

For the speed, efficiency, and good humor with which she typed the manuscript and assisted in the proof-reading, my sincere thanks to Susan Huffman--who was still Susan Stigall when she started the project! Mary Lou Baker, Betty Van Hoose and Bernice Coyle all helped with typing on parts of the book at earlier stages.

Finally, I thank my wife, Carole--for making me happy enough to write books, for everything.

CONTENTS

PREFACE

When the late, great Richard Hofstadter collected several of his essays into a volume entitled <u>The Paranoid Style in American Politics</u> in 1965, he wrote in the introduction:

> The most difficult and delicate task that faces the author of a book of essays is that of writing an introduction that makes his various pieces seem considerably more unified, in theme and argument, than they were in fact when they were written. The best case for gathering essays in a book is simply that it makes them more accessible and more permanent. The best case that can be made for the unity of any such collection is a personal and informal one, and perhaps for that reason is rarely resorted to: it is that the several parts, as the product of a single mind, have a certain stamp upon them; they must be, at least in their style of thought and their concerns, unified by some underlying intellectual intent.
> (p. vii)

It is hoped that, in addition, the essays collected here do have a unifying theme, at least a broad one. The title, <u>History and Historians</u>, is significant; the concern is with what history is, with why we should study it, and how, with how to "do" history, with some innovative approaches to history, and finally with historiography (i.e., the history of historical writing, or the study of historians and their interpretations of history). Thus, part I of this collection is an introductory essay on definitions of history, reasons for studying it, and historical method. Parts II and III approach historiography, the former through two case studies of an individual historian and the latter through several book reviews. Finally, part IV grows out of two rather successful recent experiences with "innovative" courses in history.

June, 1982   D. D. J.

I

HISTORY:

DEFINITIONS, REASONS, AND METHODS

The distinguished Harvard historian Oscar Handlin presented a paper at the 1970 annual meeting of the American Historical Association (AHA) in Boston entitled "History: A Discipline in Crisis?" Though many differed with some of his conclusions, few questioned that the appropriate response to his title was a resounding "yes." The crisis continues, and in some ways has worsened.

Handlin's paper was printed in a somewhat different form in the Summer, 1971, issue of The American Scholar. His analysis is marred by a heavy strain of nostalgia; one cannot help but question the impression he gives of the 1930's, when he first became active in the AHA, as a golden age when the historical profession had virtually no problems. But some of his points must be taken seriously. The "crisis" of which he speaks involves primarily the "dissolution of the sense of community"--sex, age, ethnic background, and ideology all divide us--and the "decay of professional standards." He could easily have added the glut of the job market in the historical profession in the past few years in all areas and and at all levels, and the threatened position of history as a discipline in the curriculum of many schools. "There is little reason to be cheerful about the status of teaching history in both the secondary schools and colleges and universities," reported a recent newsletter of the Organization of American Historians (OAH).

What can be done about the crisis? There has been a healthy concern shown by the major national organizations, like the AHA and the OAH, among other ways by including sessions in their programs on the state of the discipline, teaching, etc. At the individual campus level, we can help by introducing history as a discipline as a part of regular history courses, or as a separate course, or both. At the University of Tulsa, we created a new course. How strange, we thought, that the other social sciences all offered courses introducing their disciplines, but history did not. This situation seemed based on the assumption that students knew what they needed to know about history as a field--or, worse, that there was nothing to know about it, since history is simply an area in which you take required courses and memorize a lot of material. We began teaching "An Introduction to History" at the sophomore level in 1971; the response has been excellent. The course was divided into four major parts: (1) what is history, and why and how to study it, including some fundamentals of historical method; (2) historiography; (3) philosophy of history; and (4) the historical profession. As the course has evolved, its title has been changed to "History and Historians," and only the first two of these topics are covered extensively.

This essay is an outgrowth of that course, and deals with the first of the four parts outlined above. It begins with some brief quotations on the subject selected to provoke thought and discussion. The main body is a brief narrative of the subject at hand. There is then an annotated bibliography of some really basic titles in the area, which serves not only to show the major sources for this work, but as suggested further reading on the subject as well. It is hoped that this brief introduction will be helpful not only in similar courses, but as supplementary material in survey and other history courses as well. The style is intentionally informal, almost conversational.

HISTORY: DEFINITIONS, REASONS, AND METHODS

Food for Thought and Discussion on History

". . . . history repeats itself because no one was listening the first time." --Thomas A. Bailey

"Those who cannot remember the past are condemned to repeat it." --Santayana

Tyrone: "Mary! For God's sake, forget the past!"
Mary: "Why? How can I? The past is the present, isn't it? It's the future, too. We all try to lie out of that but life won't let us." --Eugene O'Neill (Long Day's Journey into Night)

"The worst possible enemy to society is the man who . . . is cut loose in his standards of judgment from the past; and universities which train men to use their minds without carefully establishing the connection of their thought with that of the past, are instruments of social destruction." --Woodrow Wilson

"Without a sense of history, no man can understand the problems of his times." --Winston Churchill

"I have but one lamp by which my feet are guided, and that is the lamp of experience. I know of no way of judging of the future but by the past." --Patrick Henry

"History, by apprising them [the people] of the past, will enable them to judge of the future; it will avail them of the experience of other times and other nations; it will qualify them as judges of the actions and designs of men; it will enable them to know ambition under every guise it may assume; and knowing it, to defeat its views." --Thomas Jefferson

"Let my son often read and reflect on history; this is the only true philosophy." --Napoleon

". . . . the chief lesson to be derived from a study of the past is that it holds no simple lessons--and the historian's main responsibility is to prevent anyone from claiming that it does."
--Martin Duberman

"Why do people hate, fear, and deny change? It has brought them everything they value most; it may still have wonderful things in preparation." --Lloyd J. Reynolds

"History can be well written only in a free country." --Voltaire

"Other historians relate facts to inform us of facts. You relate them to excite in our hearts an intense hatred of lying, ignorance, hypocrisy, superstition, tyranny; and the anger remains even after the memory of the facts has disappeared."
--Diderot (to Voltaire)

"A comprehension of the United States today, an understanding of the rise and progress of the forces which have made it what it is, demands that we would rework our history from the new points of view afforded by the present." --Frederick Jackson Turner

". . . . it is stultifying to celebrate the rebels of the past . . . while we silence the rebels of the present." --Henry Steele Commager

"The history of the powerless, the inarticulate, the poor has not yet begun to be written because they have been treated no more fairly by historians than they have been treated by their contemporaries." --Jesse Lemisch

"History is bunk." --Henry Ford

Definitions

History is the study of the human past with the purpose of understanding and possibly improving the human present and future.

Notice the insistence on including the statement of purpose as an integral part of the definition itself; that's probably the only part of this particular definition that might be controversial. But it seems that a study of the past without that effort to relate it to now would be a study of the past for the past's sake. That might be fun to some people, but it wouldn't be worth much, and it would be something like antiquarianism rather than history.

"The conceptions of history have been almost as numerous as the men who have written history," said the great American frontier historian Frederick Jackson Turner in 1891. It's still true; it would be extremely difficult to find one definition of history on which two historians could agree.

On the other hand, many professional historians, when asked for their working definition of history, will admit that they don't have one, or at least that they haven't thought about it in a long time. And when pressured they are likely to respond with a cop-out ("History is what historians do," "history is fun") rather than a definition, or with a definition so general ("history is the past," "history is the study of the past") that it has little practical value.

Diversity, of course, is healthy. But ignorance is not. Every historian should have his or her own working definition of history. This section should help you to develop one.

The 1971 unabridged Webster's Third New International Dictionary should be a good place to start. It has many definitions of history, but these three are most helpful:

(1) a systematic written account comprising a chronological record of events and usually including a philosophical explanation of the cause and origin of such events.

(2) a branch of knowledge that records and explains past events as steps in the sequence of human activities: the study of the character and significance of events.

(3) the events that form the subject matter of a history . . . . especially those events involving or concerned with mankind.

Notice the three different thrusts: (1) a narrative of events;

(2) a field of study; (3) the past itself.

This is closely related to the three-way definition given by Wood Gray in the widely-used reference work Historian's Handbook. History, says Gray, can be defined as happening, as record, and as field of study.

History as happening can be incredibly broad. In other words, history is everything that has happened from the beginning of time to right now. But there are limitations on this. History is ordinarily concerned only with the human past. But to say that history is everything that man has ever been, thought, said, and done is still very broad.

Which leads to history as record, and another limitation --for we cannot know everything man has ever been/thought/ said/done. "Records" for the historian usually means written records. However, from the period before the invention of writing, archaelogical finds are certainly valid sources of history. And in our time new types of sources have been provided by photographic and phonographic devices. Ironically, however, these new devices, for example the telephone, have tended to eliminate some of the written records so valuable as historical sources for earlier times.

History as field of study is rather new in the history of man. The Greek scholar Herodotus, who is usually considered "the father of history," wrote in the fifth century B. C. , but the emergence of history as an academic discipline with full status was a nineteenth century phenomenon, the result of the work of the German Leopold von Ranke and other "scientific" historians. (Of his famous dictum that the goal of history was to recreate the past "wie es eigentlich gewesen ist," or "as it actually happened," more later.) In the United States, history emerged as a separate and respectable discipline and profession during the late nineteenth and early twentieth century.

Most academic disciplines at one time or another have claimed to be "central" to all of man's knowledge, if not the first in point of time. (Philosophy, quite frankly, can probably make the best case. Without really going into it, didn't all knowledge stem from philosophy? And the ultimate degree in virtually all fields is still the Ph. D. , i. e. Doctor of Philosophy.) It doesn't really matter, since all disciplines obviously have their place and make their contribution, but history certainly can make such a claim. To be a good historian, one must have some mastery not only of history, but at times also of anthropology, archaelogy, economics, geography, journalism, philosophy, linguistics, political science, psychology, sociology, literature, etc.

Notice the diversity of those fields! And the "etc." is important too, for the list could be extended almost indefinitely. Among other things, it should impress you with the difficulty of being a good historian. But also it raises the question of whether history is a part of the humanities or a part of the social sciences. Or, as the question most frequently goes, is history an art or a science? It's like the chicken and the egg, or slavery and racism. That is, it can be discussed productively for a while, but then it becomes fruitless, for the only acceptable answer is obviously that it is neither and both.

Walter T.K. Nugent deals with this question meaningfully in his book Creative History. "Ask most historians today whether history is art or science," he writes, "and most will reply, probably, that it is scientific in its method and artistic in its execution; in other words, do your research scientifically, but write it artistically." Nugent then compares the methods and subject matter of a historian, a physicist, and a novelist with respect to a few common problems. All three begin at the same place: something needs to be explained. But the thing to be explained is very different, and so the methods must differ also. The physicist makes use of laboratory experiments, the novelist of personal observation, and the historian a diverse lot of written and oral records. Here is one way in which the historian differs from both the others, i.e., he cannot confront his subject matter directly, but must rely on sources. Thus the importance of "scientific rules of evidence" for the historian in his use of sources. As Nugent says, "He must verify his sources and combine and judge them intelligently in order to become as certain as he can that they are accurately representing the past to him."

In three other areas of comparison, Nugent finds only one in which the historian more resembles the physicist than the novelist, i.e., the question of how definite or compelling the evidence is. The novelist's evidence is in flux, the physicist's stable: "Historical evidence can very often, though not always, show with almost total certainty that some things are true and others are not true." Many historians differ with Nugent on this point.

The historian is closer to the novelist, first, in that he cannot change the conditions under which his subject matter behaves. Nugent illustrates this well and cleverly:

> The physicist can . . . find the boiling point of a new substance, for example, very definitely and accurately by boiling it a repeated number of times. The historian cannot locate the "boiling point" of revolutions in general by bringing France in 1789 or Russia in 1917 to a boil a repeated number of times. He must deal with unique occurrences.

Secondly, the historian is closer to the novelist than the physicist in mode of presentation, i.e., he is dependent more upon written language.

Again, this history as art or science argument is an interesting one. To a certain extent it can be productive; it can take on broader ramifications, for example, by making it a humanities/social sciences dichotomy. But ultimately we must realize that there is no simple or correct answer.

Indeed, there are few simple or correct answers in history. It is incredibly broad and complex. It is unique in that it is the only discipline that encompasses virtually all of the others. The very word "history" comes from the Greek word historia, "to inquire." No limits; just inquire. The nineteenth century English historian E. A. Freeman's famous dictum that "History is past politics" is far too restrictive to be acceptable to the vast majority of historians today.

History is also probably unique among the disciplines in the duality of its implications. In other words, when one hears "sociology" or "political science," one thinks of the discipline, the study of something--the study of human beings in their social relationships, or the study of man's political behavior. But when one hears "history," one may think of either "the past" or "the study of the past." In other words, history is the only discipline in which the same word commonly refers to both the discipline and the content of the discipline.

With all this breadth and complexity of history, how can it possibly be that anyone would find it uninteresting? Yet how many times have you heard some variety of such statements as "I'm not interested in history" or "History is boring"? Maybe you've said something like that yourself! Probably such an attitude results from one or more of the following three factors: (a) bad teaching in history courses the person has had; (b) misconceptions of what history is; (c) both a and b.

History doubtless continues to suffer more from poor teaching than any other discipline. This is true at all levels, but especially in our high schools. Partly it results from people teaching history who simply are not qualified to teach it--by training, by interest, or both. The standard joke is that it is taught by the coach; but it's a joke with too much truth to it to be very funny. But poor quality history teaching can also take place when the teacher is qualified, or at least theoretically qualified. The low salaries, heavy load, poor textbooks (which can't be changed for several years in many states), etc., can lead to the teaching being just as bad as if the teacher were not qualified at all.

What about the misconceptions of what history really is? It's really very closely related to poor teaching. How can anyone be expected to be excited by history if their history courses have consisted almost entirely of being forced to memorize long lists of dates, names, places, etc.? They'll come out thinking that's what history is. And they can hardly be blamed for considering that boring and irrelevant. They'll come out thinking history is dead.

There's another kind of attitude that that approach to history can inculcate which was made clear by a recent "Peanuts" comic strip. Sitting at their desks, one student asks of another: "What did you write for question number five?" The answer: "I said that he was one of our greatest presidents and one of our most beloved leaders." "Do you really believe that?" the first student asks with a shocked look. "No," the other student replies matter-of-factly, "but I've learned never to bad-mouth a president in a history test." And the look on the face of the student who asked the question shows that he understands, and that he realizes he should probably have answered in that manner also.

Memorizing things without knowing why or relating them to issues or themes of importance, in other words, does not promote critical thinking. And, quite simply, it is not history. It's not history any more than locating things on a map is geography. Learning facts, however--the building blocks of history--is a necessary step toward becoming a good historian. One cannot justifiably interpret without knowing something to interpret.

History is people, history is life. And anyone to whom that is not interesting is to be pitied, and probably belongs in some institution other than one of higher learning.

But, to conclude this section, back specifically to definitions of history. It was stated that there are about as many definitions of history as there are historians. Here are a few more which might be helpful: the purpose, remember, is to evolve a working definition of your own.

Robert V. Daniels, in an excellent little book, Studying History: How and Why, defines history briefly, but meaningfully, as "the memory of human group experience," or "the record of all experience."

Norman F. Cantor and Richard I. Schneider, in How to Study History, insist on giving three slightly different definitions. All approaches to history and all schools of thought of the twentieth century, they believe, fall under one or another of these definitions:

(1) History is the study of what men have done and said and thought in the past. (2) History is biography, that is, a work of the creative imagination in which the author attempts to recreate the life and thoughts of particular men who actually lived at a certain time. (3) History is the study of man in his social aspects

both past and present.

Finally, Donald V. Gawronski, in History: Meaning and Method, gives this definition of history, closely related to the one given at the beginning of this section: "the humanistic, interpretive study of past human society, the purpose of which is to gain insight into the present with the fervent hope of perhaps influencing a more favorable future course for the human race."

Reasons

The insistence on including purpose as part of definition leads logically to an exploration of the reasons for studying history. Howard Zinn's brilliant book, The Politics of History, includes these comments on perhaps the most commonly used cliche as to why we should study history:

> Teachers and writers of history almost always speak warmly (and vaguely) of how "studying history will help you understand our own time." This usually means the teacher will make the point quickly in his opening lecture, or the textbook will dispose of this in an opening sentence, after which the student is treated to an encyclopedic, chronological recapitulation of the past. In effect, he is told: "The past is useful to the present. Now you figure out how."

And he's right! But more of Zinn and history's relevance later.

One of America's most distinguished historians, Allan Nevins, wrote a book in 1938 (revised in 1962) entitled The Gateway to History. One chapter he called "A Proud Word for History." In any discussion of the question "Why study history?" it still deserves quoting and paraphrasing at some length. "The uses of history are almost endless," Nevins begins.

> It may be read for a hundred reasons, and when read merely for amusement, for its rich pageantry

and drama alone, it insensibly serves other
ends. But to understand its more important
values we must approach it on an elevated
level, and measure it not in relation to individuals, but to societies and nations.

We err when we instinctively think of the past when we
hear the word history, says Nevins, "for history is actually
a bridge connecting the past with the present, and pointing
the road to the future." And since mankind is "always more or
less storm-driven," history is "the sextant of states which,
tossed by wind and current, would be lost in confusion if they
could not fix their position." History helps them do this,
whether they realize it or not. In Nevins' words, it "enables
bewildered bodies of human beings to grasp their relationship with their past, and helps them chart on general lines
their immediate forward course."

And more. History not only <u>guides</u> us in our daily rounds,
it is also a <u>creator</u> of our future. As Nevins states it, "The
conception which men have of their record in generations
past shapes their dreams and ambitions for the generations
to come." So, "To give a people a full sense of their future
we need first the historians who give them a full sense of their
past."

History, then, insists Nevins, has been "a maker of
nations," and its "role as their continuing inspirer is almost
equally important."

The nature of the inspiration is highly varied,
but its central importance is this, that it tends
to make each individual a sharer in the great
deeds, ideas, and movements of his ancestors
or forerunners, and to awaken an emulative
passion in his breast. It tends also, since
history tells a very mixed tale, to awaken healthy
doubts, repulsions, and condemnations, which may
be nearly as valuable; but the positive side is
more important than the negative.

One could argue on this last point, with Hitlerian Germany
as a prime example, that history can as readily be a destroyer

14

of nations as a maker thereof. But Nevins is aware of the pitfalls of excessive nationalism in history, and insists that "The
best inspiration of history . . . outruns mere national feeling
and applies to all humanity, fortifying its higher resolves."
He also knows that "Whenever history is invoked to shape the
present and future, . . . it obviously runs very real perils,"
for "The servant of truth cannot be slave of party or nation."

Good history, says Nevins, "stands ready to give the
casual reader sound amusement, the student instruction, the
philosopher ideas, and the statesman parallels and prophecies;
ready, more importantly, to give any nation a sense of the
union of past, present, and future."

Though he does not really say it quite so simply, much of
what Nevins writes suggests that the "proud word for history"
is relevance. So, more on that subject.

Zinn, at the beginning of The Politics of History, quotes
Diderot on Voltaire: "Other historians relate facts to inform us
of facts. You relate them to excite in our hearts an intense
hatred of lying, ignorance, hypocrisy, superstition, tyranny;
and the anger remains even after the memory of the facts has disappeared." If this was true of Voltaire, it is also true of
Zinn's own work. His starting point, he says, is "the idea of
writing history in such a way as to extend human sensibilities,
not out of this book into other books, but into the going
conflict over how people shall live, and whether they shall
live." Zinn questions, then, not only the possibility but the
desirability of "neutrality" or "objectivity," and strongly and
eloquently urges "value-laden historiography." This is
obviously quite a contrast to the old von Rankean view of
history-as-chronicling. Zinn suggests five critieria for
radical history, which he clearly feels apply to all history, "five
ways in which history can be useful." The first is that history
can intensify, expand, and sharpen our perception of how bad
things are for the victims of the world. Second, "We can
expose the pretensions of governments to either neutrality
or beneficence." Third, we can expose the ideology (i.e., the
"rationale for the going order") that pervades our culture.
Fourth, "We can recapture those few moments in the past
which show the possibility of a better way of life than that which
has dominated the earth thus far." And, finally, "We can show

15

how good social movements can go wrong, how leaders can betray their followers, how rebels can become bureaucrats, how ideals can become frozen and reified."

A large portion of Zinn's book consists of some case studies on class, race, and nationalism in which he attempts to begin to meet these criteria; he has tried it in some of his other works as well, for example SNCC: The New Abolitionists, and Vietnam: The Logic for Withdrawal.

Another advocate of current social relevance as the yard-stick of history is Staughton Lynd, who in 1967 made an elo-quent plea for "The Historian as Participant." Differing with the traditional view that considerable time should pass after events before the historian can deal with them in proper per-spective, Lynd argues that the historian's "first duty" is the "sensitive chronicling in depth of the important events of his own lifetime." And the second task, hardly a familiar one to most historians either, is "the projection of alternative futures on the basis of the richness of the experience of the past." This "is not to predict but to envision, to say (as Howard Zinn has put it) not what will be but what can be." Lynd has put his beliefs to work admirably in both his writings and his activities. He was deeply involved in both the civil rights and anti-Vietnam movements, and more recently has worked on an oral history project on radicalism in the labor movement. Lynd, then, argues that not only history but the historian must be "relevant."

If history is so relevant, why don't more students realize that it has some meaning for their lives? So much has been said, and with some justification, about the lack of historical-mindedness on the part of today's youth; they are such prison-ers of the present. To the extent that that is true, part of the blame lies, again, with teachers of history. But part of it lies also in a too-stringent understanding of the word "relevant" by many college students in recent years. Some-one in journalism commented recently that we spend too much of our time poring over the past and need to study things like computers and race relations. Foolishness! The question of computers is a whole different thing, but how can anyone possibly approach an understanding of race relations in this country today without first having some understanding of the experience of black people in slavery, Civil War, and Reconstruction? Many students were helped to a healthy questioning attitude toward this country's involvement in Southeast Asia by learning in history courses that the cliches about our wars--we always had justifiable, possibly even holy motives for entering them, we always won, etc.--were just not true. We did not "win" the War of 1812, for example, and it is extremely difficult to justify our behavior toward Mexico in 1846. But all this does not mean that history teachers, in order to be relevant, must conclude their lectures on these subjects with advice on what students should do about today's problems. That would be carrying the idea of relevance to a ridiculous extreme, and it would also be going considerably beyond the limits of history. A study of the Peloponnesian Wars, you see, can be just as relevant as the study of the role of minorities in this country or of diplomatic history, if approached properly, i.e., from the perspective of understanding what makes people behave the way they do, what causes wars, etc.

History, let it be clearly asserted here, with all its relevance, is not going to save the world. No academic discipline is going to do that. Two graduate students, one in literature and the other in sociology, were involved in a conversation recently. The first was working on a thesis on some rather obscure early twentieth century English novelist, the second on something locally about problems of the aging. The sociology student kept giving the English student a rough time about being irrelevant; "We're going to save the world, and what are you doing?" was the general thrust of the argument. Finally, the person in literature said angrily, and meaningfully, "Alright, you save the world--and we'll make it worth living in!" That ended the conversation. Why relate it here? Perhaps it is not too much to suggest that history might make some small contribution to both.

A final point on relevance--actually something of a fantasy--then a cautionary note, or limitation. You know the old argument about what makes history--men, God, inexorable historical forces, accident, etc.? The answer is really quite simple: historians make history. History is what historians say it is. It sort of gives you a feeling of power, being a historian. Maybe that's a whole separate reason from relevance for studying history.

17

The cautionary word about relevance comes from Martin Duberman: ". . . . the chief lesson to be derived from a study of the past is that it holds no simple lesson--and the historian's main responsibility is to prevent anyone from claiming that it does." He was concerned most, of course, about the common habit of so many non-historians, policitians and journalists especially, to proclaim that "history shows that. . . . " or "history proves . . . . " or "the lesson of history in this case is . . . . " And his warning is well taken.

There are so many reasons for studying history besides relevance. Unfortunately, the answer most likely to be given by students when asked "Why study history?" is "Because it's required." And, of course, it is. Most states and/or institutions of higher learning require a basic survey in United States history and/or western civilization. But why is it required, that's the question. What are some of the other reasons, then, for studying history?

Nevins eloquently touched upon some of the traditional ones, having to do with the value, individually and collectively, of the broad liberal arts/humanities/social studies background of which history is a part. Walter T. K. Nugent also deals meaningfully with the reasons for studying history, including specifically the question of why it is required.

Even the question "Why study history?" can be interpreted in two different ways, Nugent points out. One is in the sense of "How can it help me make a living?" Here Nugent discusses the various occupations and professions for which historical training is helpful. And, of course, this is quite appropriate; but the second way the question "Why study history?" can be interpreted is more relevant here: "How can it help me become a better person?" Interestingly and convincingly, Nugent argues that this question, though it seems at first less practical and more abstract, is really more practical than the first: "Since making a living is only one part of life, but living with oneself as a person is, for better or worse, full-time, the second question is the more practical, since it affects one much more profoundly and much more often." Nugent's answer to the second question is interesting. It's all summed up in two quotations, he says. The first is from the English poet Alexander Pope: 'Know then theyself, presume not God to scan;

18

the proper study of mankind is man." The second is from the
Greek playwright Menander: "In many ways the saying 'Know
thyself' is not well said. It were more practical to say 'Know
other people.' " Concludes Nugent: "Nowhere do you study
more people in more varied circumstances than in history.
Everyone is a product of his society; every society is a product
of its past. To know the past and that of other people is to
know yourself. "

Nugent sees other reasons for studying history. It
"releases you from the prison of your own time and place. " It
"teaches us lessons that may help us avoid in the future some of
the mistakes we have made in the past. " It has "the virtue of
being able to train us to think. " And, finally, "no other subject
pulls together all of human experience so broadly, and no other
subject relates the many parts of this experience to each other. "

Nugent concludes his "Why Study History?" chapter, as he
does each one, with some questions and exercises. Portions
of this one might be helpful here. "Name some fields of study
which are useful for training a person to do some particular
thing, and, then, name some fields useful for helping a person
be a certain kind of person. " The first type Nugent would call
"training, " the second type "education. " "Is there a distinction,
then, " he continues, "between training and education? Is
education practical? " And the crucial question: "Is history a
subject that trains, or is it one that educates, or is it both? "

On the issue of history being required, Nugent poses these
thought-provoking questions:

> Why do you think history is required, or at least
> strongly suggested, for successful completion of
> primary, secondary, and college curricula in this
> and other countries? Can you suggest some practical
> reason, or do you attribute this practice to the sheer
> inertia of tradition?

In his Historian's Handbook, Wood Gray suggests that any
of three possible responses should give an adequate answer to the
question "Why study history?" and that together "they should be
irrefutable:" (1) as literature, (2) as vicarious experience,
(3) as professional training. The third is self-explanatory; the

19

second is really the kind of thing we have already dealt with in terms of history aiding in a general way in understanding the present and improving the future. Gray's comments on history as literature deserve quotation:

> For at least twenty-four centuries written history has stood as a major literary form. Effectively presented, it has the ability to depict the unfolding of fateful events and to portray the rise or deterioration of character in a manner that ranks it with great novels and epic poetry. This function of history makes it incumbent on every historian, whether an experienced practitioner writing a book or the neophyte preparing a class paper, to cultivate a style worthy of his theme. Oral presentation carries comparable responsibilities.

Robert V. Daniels' Studying History: How and Why, is convincing and at times even eloquent in its message. "History deserves to be studied out of curiosity if nothing else," Daniels insists. But that is by no means the only reason he gives in the chapter on "The Uses of History." "A person must know some history even to begin to understand the world he or she lives in, or to act with any wisdom and perspective." Daniels is also well aware, however, that the "lessons of history" thing can be over-done--and frequently is. History does not repeat itself: "even two like events differ in that the first has no precedent, while the second has. But even in this respect history can teach a lesson--nothing ever stays the same." History has innate value in developing thinking, curiosity, reason, communication, skepticism, objectivity, and, above all, perspective and "the detachment tha t enables the observer to rise above human conflicts and see all sides of a question, no matter which position one personally prefers." A question like "Who was right in the American Civil War, the North or the South?" is meaningless, Daniels insists, because "right" depends on setting in time and so many subjective factors. Either-or judgments, Daniels correctly points out, are "an affront to historical reality." People are not that simple; their history cannot be either. Good historical study, concludes Daniels, "appreciates how rarely, if ever, clear-cut conflicts occur between good and evil, black and white. . . . This is the most important lesson that history can offer its students for

20

coping with their own world. "

Finally, Daniels clarifies the relationship between history and citizenship. Pointing out that one of the major tasks, and opportunities, of teaching is "to prepare the student to be an informed and conscientious citizen, to play his part as a responsible member of a democratic society, " Daniels says that history can probably contribute more to this than any other discipline. But since this is closely related to the tendency for history to be regarded as "the natural vehicle for teaching the private citizen the public virtues of loyalty and responsibility, " there is frequently a contradiction between this and history as training in detachment, objectivity, and critical thinking.

In other words, we have been talking about the uses of history in this section; there are also abuses, which have only been hinted at. Three of the most frequent ones, and they overlap, are history-as-patriotism, history-as-propaganda, and the lessons-of-history syndrome.

So, study history to make a living, to broaden your mind, because it's fun, because it helps you learn how to think, because it's relevant . . . .

Try to re-think the reasons dealt with in this section, and maybe come up with some of your own.

Methods

It should be kept clearly in mind that how to study, history or any other subject, is a highly individualized thing. There is no single "right" way to study. Some general suggestions might be helpful, but you will doubtless need to modify them to suit yourself.

First, some practical suggestions on how to study for a history course, then some basic guidelines for the two most common forms of historical writing students are expected to do, book reviews and research papers.

Norman F. Cantor and Richard I. Schneider point out

21

correctly in <u>How to Study History</u> that one of the basic pre-
requisites for studying history is an open mind. How strange,
then, that so much of our teaching emphasizes rote memoriza-
tion, which obviously is more likely to promote a closed mind
than an open one. This situation is due at least partially to the
examination system. Faced with large classes and the necessity
of providing an exact rating of a student's attainment, the professor turns to "objective" exams: true-false, multiple choice,
matching, fill-in-the-blanks. It's very difficult to avoid tricky,
obscure questions, and many teachers don't even try. Students
react to this by reluctantly cramming in everything they can,
which they then regurgitate on the exam. Frequently, they don't
find out which questions they missed, much less why--and by
this point they probably don't care.

It doesn't have to be that bad. Wood Gray and Cantor and
Schneider both provide some suggestions for studying history
that might prove helpful. This is a paraphrase of Gray's nine-
step guide: (1) Prepare and conscientiously follow a planned
schedule of two or three-hour study sessions throughout each
week at a time when you will be alert and in a place relatively
free from distraction. (2) After getting acquainted with a book
by skimming, read through the assigned portions at fiction-
reading speed in order to grasp the over-all theme and content.
(3) Re-read it more thoroughly for details. (4) While reading it
thoroughly, or just after, prepare a brief outline of each
assignment or chapter. (5) In the margin of your outline, make
a list of the more important facts. (6) Repeat this process for
your notes on each class lecture. (7) Review your outlines at
least weekly, "being sure that you grasp the relationship
between the facts and the larger patterns of interpretation."
(8) Re-read those portions of your book and/or notes which your
review reveals to you are vague in your mind. (9) Make out
sample examination questions, and answer them.

Again, remember that there is no magical formula.
Cantor and Schneider, who give some suggestions similar to
Gray's, are aware that they might seem "trivial" and
"superfluous" to some students. But you do need <u>some</u> systematic method, and the suggestions here might help you to
develop a workable system of your own.

Some suggestions on taking and using lecture notes might

be of value, these from Cantor and Schneider: (1) Take down only the major points, especially the interpretive ones and those not in the reading. (Notice that you should do the reading before-hand!) The point is that it is very easy to get so bogged down in the mechanics of taking down every word that you miss much of the substance of the lecture. (2) Immediately after a lecture, force yourself to summarize its major theme in just a few lines. (3) Within twenty-four hours, write a brief summary of the lecture in your own words. (4) It's a good idea to leave a rather wide margin on one side of your notes to allow room for comments of various kinds.

Some of these suggestions should prove useful whether you are taking essay examinations or "objective" ones. The basic difference is that for the objective test your emphasis almost has to be more on specific factual material, while for the essay you think in broader terms with the facts helping you to illustrate themes or trends or interpreations.

Finally, it simply cannot be emphasized too much that all this varies greatly with each individual student and professor. Perhaps the only safe advice to give in every case is that given by Harvard's A. B. Hart many years ago. Hart, in turn, credited one of his German history professors with these "three rules" of historical study: (1) Read. (2) Read widely. (3) Read very widely. History, in whatever area and at whatever level, requires a great deal of reading. You should take whatever steps necessary to develop your speed and retention as fully as possible.

There's considerable latitude as to the "right" way to write a book review and a research paper in history, also, but perhaps not quite so much as in the every-day procedures of taking a course.

Many history professors, especially in advanced courses, will require the writing of book reviews. Bear in mind that a book review is different from a book report. While the latter is usually primarily a summary of the contents of the book, the book review is an evaluation. It should begin with a full bibliographical citation of the book being reviewed, i. e., author, title, place, publisher, and date, and is usually expected to be approximately two or three typewritten pages in length. There might be a very brief summary, but usually not; factual material is ordinarily brought into the review only to the extent necessary to make clear the interpretation of the author and/or the evaluative point being made by the reviewer. In other words, some of the central questions which a review should attempt to answer about a book are: What, if anything, is the author's thesis or interpretation? (In some books, of course, there might not be a clear-cut thesis or interpretation, but there should at least be some purpose that the author makes clear.) Is it valid? Are the author's sources, methods, style, etc., adequate for what he is attempting to do? More simply stated: Is the book good or bad? Why? What are its good points and bad points? What contribution does the book make to its field?

All this should make it obvious that good book reviewing is not really a simple task. The beginning student is frequently reluctant to attempt an evaluation along the lines suggested above, and might be inclined to lapse into the easier task of summarizing the book. But, as Cantor and Schneider say, "No matter how famous the book being considered is, no matter how learned the author may appear and how uninformed about the subject the student himself may feel, it should always be remembered that the desired goal is an evaluation, a critique of the book and not merely a report of the book's contents." It's an experience that you need to have, an ability that you need to develop, so launch into it. If you feel especially uncertain, you might try reading a few book reviews in good journals like the American Historical Review or the Journal of American History to see what they're like--though certainly not all the ones that appear there are well-done. And your professor will usually be glad to talk with you about the specific book you are reviewing, which might help you to feel confident that your ideas are not too far afield.

The biggest and most difficult task you will be expected to undertake in an undergraduate history course is the writing of a research paper, or, as some prefer to call it, a term paper. The Ph. D. dissertation is a step above the Master's thesis, which is a step above the graduate seminar paper, which is a step above the undergraduate research paper. So the development of some of the fundamentals of sound historical method very

24

early in the undergraduate career is crucial, especially if one contemplates higher work in history. Even if not, it is a valuable experience.

It can also be a very grueling task. Writing a research paper is a small-scale exercise in what creative history is all about: bringing together sources, synthesizing, and coming up with conclusions of your own. Most instructors don't expect it to be anything profound or original. It can be extremely educational, and even fun, especially if you are really interested in your topic.

An over-view: normally the research paper is expected to be 12 to 15 double-spaced type-written pages in length, with at least 10 or 12 sources in the bibliography, mechanically near-perfect, and with footnote and bibliographical references properly done.

Specifically, it should be helpful here to make brief comments and suggestions on selecting a topic, finding sources, taking notes, making an outline, writing, proper form for footnotes and bibliography, and the final order in which the various portions of the paper should appear.

Two basic criteria should be used in the selection of a topic. The first is interest. If you are not interested in the subject you choose, it will be extremely difficult for you to put yourself into it with enough enthusiasm to do a decent paper. The second is availability of an adequate amount of source material. We suggest 10 or 12 sources as the minimum: these might be books, articles, newspapers, documents, films, interviews, or whatever. But if you don't have at least that many, probably you cannot justify a paper of the suggested length because you simply will not have an adequate number of sources to give you the proper perspective.

Two further comments on the selection of a topic: (1) Usually your instructor will need to approve of your topic before you really go to work on it. (2) The most frequent problem for undergraduate students of history in topic selection is coming up with one that is workable within the time and space limitations set. In other words, to use an extreme example, "The Life and Times of Adolph Hitler" is pretty obviously a bit much for the kind of paper we're concerned with here. Topics which are too broad are chosen far more often than topics which are too narrow; the primary way the latter might happen is if your library simply doesn't have the material. Your instructor can usually be of help on this issue of proper breadth of your topic.

Selecting a topic, then, gets you involved right away in the second step of writing a research paper, finding sources, since you will need to check at least far enough on sources to see that they are adequate before really settling down on a topic. The primary limitation on sources will be the holdings of your library. Though you should be aware of the Inter-Library Loan system of which most college and university libraries are members, making it possible to borrow from other libraries, undergraduates are expected to use this service sparingly if at all at most institutions.

Finding sources is a crucial part of writing a research paper. If you don't find an adequate number of good sources, you can't produce a good paper--it's really that simple. The library is to the historian what the laboratory is to the scientist. Become thoroughly at home in it! The card catalog is the starting point. Most libraries use either the Dewey decimal system or the Library of Congress system. Figure out which yours is, and become thoroughly familiar with the appropriate parts of your library.

There are so many different ways to find sources that all we can do is simply list some here. Try them all; and you may think of others. Remember, once you have decided on a topic, it is your responsibillity to make use of all the appropriate sources available to you. Here are some suggestions, in addition to the card catalog, that you definitely should not miss: suggestions from your instructor; suggestions from reference librarians; the bibliography of your textbook; the bibliography and footnotes of every book that you find through any other source; journal articles; magazine articles (most important ones are indexed in the Reader's Guide to Periodical Literature); and bibliographical guides (like the Harvard Guide to American History, Bibliography of English Translations from Medieval Sources, A Select List of Works on Europe Overseas, 1715-1815, etc.--there's an excellent 40-page list of such aids in the chapter on "Pursuit of Evidence" in Wood Gray's Historian's Handbook).

It should be noted here that sources are of two basic types, primary and secondary. Most simply defined, primary sources are first-hand sources, i. e. , sources contemporary with the events you are studying, while secondary sources are accounts which are written later. A letter from George Washington to Sally Fairfax is a primary source; an article in the Journal of Southern History on the scandals of Washington's private life is a secondary source. Most undergraduate research papers in history probably will be restricted to secondary sources. However, if you can select a topic which will allow you to make use of primary sources, the experience will be worth a great deal. One way you might manage to do so is by selecting a local topic. Then you can get into newspapers for sure, probably some archival manuscripts, and possibly even interviews with people who were there if you're dealing with something recent enough. (If you do get into interviewing, have prepared questions to seek information on specific points and to keep the interview from wandering, and remember that you should be cautious in drawing conclusions from the memories of the elderly, as they are likely to become increasingly unreliable and, especially, embellished, with age.)

There is another way you might get into primary sources-- many primary sources are printed. For example, if you're working on the American Civil War, many libraries have the Official Records of the War of the Rebellion. Don't assume that a primary source is automatically a "better" source; a newspaper editorial of 1916 on the presidential election of that year is not likely to be nearly as helpful, for example-- certainly not nearly as objective--as a good article on the election fifty years later in the Journal of American History. But primary sources do give you the "feel" of history as nothing else can; it's an experience you should have as soon as possible in your historical career.

Once you have selected a topic and found your sources, the note-taking process begins. This is one of those highly-individualized steps in historical method. However, there are certain basic suggestions which should prove useful to the beginner.

Almost everyone agrees that 3" x 5" note cards should be used for bibliography. Agreement is not that common on research notes, but most seem to have good luck with 5" x 8" cards. Regardless of what size or type of material you take notes on, use the same size consistently; if you have notes on 3" x 5" cards, 5" x 8" cards, notebook paper, etc., you will have incredible problems of organization. Most research manuals will tell you to have only one main item on each note. That can get you an awfully large file of notes. However, you should either do it that way or realize that you will have to do a lot of shuffling. Don't take notes with a pencil--they'll smudge. Be sure to identify each note completely by source and page.

Probably the most common problem for the beginning undergraduate student of history in the note-taking process is determining how many notes to take. Don't take down facts which are common knowledge or which you already know; and paraphrase rather than quote unless the quote is something dramatic or interpretive which you might want to use in your paper. On the other hand, don't over-abbreviate something-- or not take it down at all!--and think you can remember it; if you're using an adequte number of sources, you probably can't.

Above all, don't try to write a research paper without taking notes! Everybody knows it can be done, but it almost always produces a very poor paper, and your instructor can almost always tell. Even if you get by with it, what has it gained you? If you're a serious student of history, the experience of developing a working system of your own is crucial.

By the time you have done your reading and note-taking, you will probably have a rough outline in your mind of what you want to do in your paper. Write it down. There's no mystical formula for outlining; just write down the major points you want to cover. For a paper of 12-15 pages length, the outline should probably be no more than one page. It may change as you go along, but without it your writing will be directionless and will probably progress much more slowly. Many instructors will want to see your outline before you start writing; even if it's not required, it might be bene- ficial to you to have it checked, especially if it's your first research paper.

Good writing, historical or otherwise, is an art. Some people have it naturally, while others don't. Most of those who don't can develop it. There's not much space to give to it here, so if you have exceptional problems, turn to one of the best works on the subject, like William Strunk and E. B. White's The Elements of Style; indeed, it's good to have a copy around for reference anyway.

A few comments here might help you avoid some of the most common problems. Most of the time, especially if you're new at writing, you're better off to write in simple, direct sentences-- one of the most common professorial notations on the margin of student papers is "not a sentence" or "awkward." Be careful of excessively long and/or excessively short paragraphs. Keep in mind the old topic sentence idea that you must have learned somewhere along the line; you don't have to stick with it strictly, but it helps not to stray too far from it. Most professors will want you to avoid first person and contractions in formal writing--"I don't think George Washington was a very good president" is a definite no-no. Be careful to avoid too many quotes and/or footnotes. In addition to indicating that you probably haven't absorbed your research very well, it is most unpleasant to read a paper which consists of other peoples' ideas and words chained together. There's no universally-accepted rule, but it might be a good idea to average somewhere around three footnotes per page. Anything more probably means your contribution to your paper is practically nil; much less probably means you have relied too much on too few sources. And in a paper of 12 to 15 pages length, any more than three or four block quotations--i. e., those more than three or four lines which are single-spaced and indented from both margins rather than placed in quotation marks--is probably excessive.

Your bibliography is the last thing in your paper. It consists of a list of the sources you have used in writing the paper. If you have used primary sources, you will want to divide your bibliography into primary and secondary sources; otherwise, a simple alphabetical isting is usually adequate. Your footnotes are your specific references for quotes and other people's ideas. (There are also "explanatory" footnotes. It's when you want to say something further on a point, but don't wish to include it in your main text. Use them sparingly.) It is not necessary that everything in your bibliography be footnoted in your paper, since some sources may have been of assistance to you in a general way only. However, you should avoid "padding" your bibliography by listing things in it that were not used at all; that will be obvious to a discerning reader.

"Proper" form for footnote and bibliographical references is a touchy subject. Instructors are ordinarily very particular about it. The problem is that you seldom find two who are particular in the same way. The form suggested here is quite widely accepted.

Most of you will use written books, edited books, articles in scholarly journals, articles in popular magazines, and articles in newspapers. Examples of proper bibliographical (B.) and footnote (F.) citations are given for each.

B.   Zinn, Howard. <u>The Politics of History.</u>
       Boston: Beacon Press, 1970.

F.   [1]Howard Zinn, <u>The Politics of History</u>
       (Boston: Beacon Press, 1970), p. 30.

B.   Borden, Morton, ed. <u>America's Ten Greatest</u>
       <u>Presidents.</u> Chicago: Rand McNally
       and Company, 1961.

F.   [1]Morton Borden, ed. <u>America's Ten</u>
       <u>Greatest Presidents</u> (Chicago: Rand McNally
       and Company, 1961), p. 159.

B.   Knight, John. "Matchless Magellan: The Story
       of a Voyage," <u>The Middle States Historical</u>
       <u>Journal,</u> XXXII (April, 1927), pp. 508-527.

F.   [1]John Knight, "Matchless Magellan: The Story
       of a Voyage," <u>The Middle States Historical Journal,</u>
       XXXII (April, 1927), p. 521.

B.   Marshall, S. L. A. "The Fight at Monkey." <u>Harper's</u>
       <u>Magazine,</u> November, 1966, pp. 111-122.

F.   [1]S. L. A. Marshall, "The Fight at Monkey,"
       <u>Harper's Magazine,</u> November, 1966, p. 113.

B. New York Times, August 15, 1945 - June 19, 1953.

F. [1]New York Times, January 13, 1947, sec. 5, p. F12.

If you use types of sources not covered here--and you well may, as these are only the most basic ones--try Kate Turabian, A Manual for Writers of Term Papers, Theses, and Dissertations. You may even use some sources not covered there. If so, consult with your instructor.

There are a lot of fancy Latin abbreviations that can be used in footnotes. Quite frankly, with one exception, they're more trouble than they're worth. The one exception is "Ibid.," meaning "in the same place." To illustrate--you've just used the article by Marshall mentioned above as footnote number one, and want to refer to it again in footnote number two:

[2] Ibid.

Or, if the second reference is to a different page:

[2] Ibid., p. 121.

Many instructors don't mind short titles in addition to or instead of Ibid. To illustrate--you've just used the article by Knight mentioned above as footnote number one, and want to refer to it again in footnote number two:

[2] Knight, "Matchless Magellan," p. 522.

It might make more sense to use Ibid. if the source is used twice in a row, but the short title if another reference intervenes.

Regardless of whose rules you follow, be clear, complete, and consistent in your references, and, when in doubt, check with your instructor.

So, you've selected a topic, built your bibliography, taken your notes, and outlined and written your paper with all the footnotes and bibliographical references in proper form. It's time for typing. Only one suggestion on that here; most profs

31

expect it to be near-perfect, so if you can't do it, hire it done.

The final order in which the various portions of the paper should appear is as follows:

(1) Title page--If you wish, be creative as to design, but be sure it includes the title, your name, the course, and the date.

(2) Preface--It may be an introduction, a foreword, or whatever, but there should be some sort of introductory remarks. Acknowledgements can go here too if you wish to make any.

(3) Table of contents--This is merely a list of the various portions of the paper, with page references showing where each part begins.

(4) Body--This is your paper. (By the way, don't list it as "Body" on the table of contents--use the title!)

(5) Footnotes--Notice! Footnotes go in as a separate section only if your instructor is nice enough not to insist that they go at the bottom of the page--ask!

(6) Bibliography.

Suggestions for Reading

This section is designed to serve two purposes. First, it is to let you know what sources have been most helpful for the writing of this work. Second, it is to suggest a few of the best things available for further reading and/or reference on the topics covered herein.

Block, Jack. Understanding Historical Research: A Search for Truth. Glen Rock, New Jersey: Research Publications, 1971.

Cantor, Norman F., and Richard I. Schneider. How to Study History. New York: Thomas Y. Crowell Company, 1967.

Daniels, Robert V. Studying History: How and Why. Third
    Edition. Englewood Cliffs, New Jersey: Prentice-Hall,
    Incorporated, 1981.

Doubleday, Neal Frank. Writing the Research Paper. Revised
    Edition. Lexington, Massachusetts: D.C. Heath and
    Company, 1971.

Gawronski, Donald V. History: Meaning and Method. Third
    Edition. Glenview, Illinois: Scott, Foresman and
    Company, 1975.

Gray, Wood, and others. Historian's Handbook: A Key to
    the Study and Writing of History. Second Edition.
    Boston: Houghton Mifflin Company, 1964.

Nevins, Allan. The Gateway to History. New, revised,
    edition. Garden City, New York: Anchor Books, 1962.

Nugent, Walter T.K. Creative History. Second Edition.
    Philadelphia: J.B. Lippincott Company, 1973.

Strunk, William, and E.B. White. The Elements of Style.
    Third Edition. New York: Macmillan Company, 1978.

Turabian, Kate L. A Manual for Writers of Term Papers,
    Theses, and Diessertations. Fourth Edition. Chicago:
    The University of Chicago Press, 1973.

Zinn, Howard. The Politics of History. Boston: Beacon
    Press, 1970.

For the section on definitions, Block, Cantor and
Schneider, Daniels, Gawronski, Gray, Nevins, and Nugent
were all helpful. Gawronski's little book has a chapter called
"A Definition of History" which is very useful, as it shows his
own definition evolving. Indeed, Gawronski deals with an
amazing amount of material in a short space. In 122 pages,
in addition to his definition of history, he treats philosophy
of history, historical method, and historiography--and all
fairly well, too, considering the limitations of space.

Nevins and Zinn were the two most helpful works for

reasons for studying history. Quite simply, they should both be read by any serious student of history. Nevins' work, originally written in 1938, has indeed provided a "gateway to history" for many students. Zinn's book might do so for more students now.

For methods, Cantor and Schneider, and Nugent are most useful for their suggestions on studying for history courses, writing book reviews, etc., while Gray and Turabian are basic for writing research papers. Block is a little-known but good guide to historical method similar to Gray, while Doubleday is another guide like Turabian not limited by discipline.

Daniels is an excellent little book which should definitely be read. So should Nugent, though it is marred somewhat by the end-of-chapter exercises, which many students seem to consider overly simplistic and patronizing.

II

AN AMERICAN HISTORIAN:

EDWARD CHANNING

There are several different possible approaches to take to writing a historiographical paper. One is to treat the different interpretations of a particular topic--the historiography of the Kansas-Nebraska Act, for example, or Andrew Jackson in American historical writing. Frank Otto Gatell and Allen Weinstein have edited an excellent (though dated--1968) anthology of such pieces under the title American Themes: Essays in Historiography. A second approach is to deal with a group of historians or a "school" of thought--the romantic historians, or the Imperial school of colonial history. The third common approach is to study an individual historian. The two essays in this section are examples of the latter.

The historian is Edward Channing. The first essay is a brief general assessment, written for a somewhat more "popular" journal--thus the absence of footnotes. The second was presented as a paper at the annual meeting of the Southern Historical Association in 1979 in a session on "Historians and Black History." Other papers were a treatment of Carter G. Woodson's role in the institutionalization of black history and a comparison of C. Vann Woodward and Ulrich B. Phillips. The critic assigned to the session dealt rather severely with all the papers, especially mine. His major complaint seemed to be that I had not been hard enough on Edward Channing for being a racist. I feel that I made it amply clear that Channing was a racist, and that that racism, for today, must be condemned. But moral indignation, while appealing at an emotional level, contributes little to the historian's craft; the soap-box is seldom an appropriate place for the historian. Besides, what does it accomplish to point the accusatory finger at a historical figure--or in this case a historian? I have left the paper unchanged.

AMERICAN HISTORIAN: EDWARD CHANNING, 1856-1931

There is a well-known story that Edward Channing was once approached by a student who said, "My father wished me to inquire what relation you were to the great Channing." He doubtless had in mind William Ellery Channing, the founder of American Unitarianism, who was indeed Edward Channing's great uncle. Channing's response, however, delivered with a characteristic thump on the chest as he peered over his rimless glasses, was "I am the great Channing!" Channing's students habitually referred to his major contribution, the six-volume History of the United States, as the "Great Work"--and so did he. Though all this may appear a bit egotistical, it is certainly true that in the field of American historical writing, Edward Channing and his History are both thoroughly deserving of the label "great."

Channing was born in 1856 in Dorchester, Massachusetts, the son of the poet Ellery Channing and Ellen Kilshaw Fuller, who was the sister of the famous journalist, critic, and social reformer, Margaret Fuller. The Channings were related to many of the well-known families in Massachusetts and New England history, such as the Higginsons, Cabots, Lowells, and Emersons. As Edward Channing once wrote, he was "related more or less to all the 'Highnesses'." Left alone at the tender age of three months by his mother's death and his father's desertion, young Edward spent most of his rather frail boyhood living at various places in and around Boston with his grandfather, Dr. Walter Channing, and Aunt Barbara.

Channing entered Harvard in the fall of 1874 and graduated in 1878 with honors in history. Two years later he received the Ph. D., with a dissertation on the Louisiana Purchase. While at Harvard, Channing studied under both Henry Adams and Henry Cabot Lodge. Though not too impressed with the latter, Channing never lost the high regard he had for Adams, for he credited Adams with leading him into the study of history as his life's work and referred to him as "the greatest teacher I have ever encountered." By the time he received the Ph. D., Channing knew definitely what he wanted to do--teach United States history at Harvard. But his application to President Charles William Eliot for such a position received the reply that there was none, along with a comment that well described the academic status of the field at that time. Eliot told Channing his desire to teach American history was "laudable;" but he cautioned of "the practical necessity of having other strings to your bow." There were only two colleges in the country, to his knowledge, where much was made of American history, he said, "and you know how elementary the teaching on that subject is in American schools. History is generally taught by a master who has several other subjects on his hands."

Channing did not give up on his goal; he merely postponed it. After an extended tour of Europe, he spent approximately two years writing book reviews and articles, all the time keeping his eyes open for possibilities in the Harvard history department. Aided by his dissertation director, Professor Henry W. Torrey, Channing received an appointment at the instructor level in 1883. His first assignment was aiding Torrey in a course on the history of treaties; only gradually, as his prestige increased and as his rival within the department, A. B. Hart, moved more and more into government, did Channing get to take over the United States history courses he really wanted to teach. He was promoted to Assistant Professor in 1887, Professor in 1897, McLean Professor of Ancient and Modern History in 1912, and was awarded Emeritus status in 1929.

Channing's advance through the academic ranks was doubtless assisted by his publishing career, which began in 1883, the same year as his teaching. He won the Robert N. Toppan Prize of $250 for an essay entitled "Town and County Government in the English Colonies." Published the following year as a volume in the Johns Hopkins University Studies in Historical and Political Science, this little work also helped get Channing elected to the elite Massachusetts Historical Society, and he presented it in briefer form as the first paper at the first meeting of the American Historical Association at Saratoga, New York, in 1884.

The Guide to the Study of American History, done in association with Hart and published in 1897, was Channing's first really major work. In that same year an excellent little volume in the Cambridge Historical Series came out, dealing with the United States between 1765 and 1865. By this time, Channing had already published another volume in the Johns

Hopkins series, an English history text co-authored with
Thomas Wentworth Higginson (Channing's cousin, who achieved
some fame as the colonel of a Black regiment in the Civil War),
and numerous articles; he also had begun with Hart, in 1892,
the editing of the series of documents they called American
History Leaflets: Colonial and Constitutional. Professor
Channing's major textbook, A Student's History of the United
States, was first published in 1897, and went through four more
editions by 1924. He also wrote several other texts for various
levels. The Jeffersonian System, 1801-1811 was Channing's
contribution to Hart's famous American Nation Series.
Channing also co-authored a history of the Great Lakes with
Marion Florence Lansing in 1909; and Frederick Jackson
Turner's name was added to those of Channing and Hart for a
new edition of the Guide in 1912. The 1897 and 1912 guides were
predecessors to the indispensable 1954 Harvard Guide to
American History, which was dedicated to Channing, Hart, and
Turner, "Who Blazed the Way."

Once he began the Great Work, Channing took little time
for anything else. (A Widener Library attendant asked
Channing one Saturday morning if he planned to attend Harvard's
football game that afternoon. His indignant response was that he
planned to labor on his Great Work until the library closed--
then go home and work some more!) Beginning in 1905, the
installments appeared at approximately four-year intervals
until the Pulitzer Prize-winning sixth volume, dealing with the
Civil War era, was published in 1925. After that, it became
obvious that Channing's age was slowing him down considerably.
He still had not finished volume VII when he died of a cerebral
hemorrhage on January 7, 1931--only the night before he had
still been working on the History!

"The most eminent of contemporary American writers of
United States history is gone," said the Boston Herald the next
day. Arthur M. Schlesinger recalled that during the hour of the
funeral, held in Harvard's Appleton Chapel, "all classes were
suspended, a tribute accorded no one else during my connection
with Harvard." Schlesinger and Samuel Eliot Morison were
among the fellow historians who served as ushers. Morison
wrote this tribute shortly thereafter:

Channing accomplished what no man had done before,

41

and what is not likely to be done again. Between his fortieth and his seventieth year, with his own hand, and from his own research, he wrote a great history of the United States from the beginning of colonization to the close of the Civil War. In the meantime, he trained scores of men to carry on the work in his own spirit of thorough and fearless inquiry; and to thousands more he imparted a love of our country's history, based on knowledge. For this he sacrificed much that men hold dear; but gained what was more dear to him: recognition, and affection. The little motherless boy, who for want of a companion created an imaginary "Mr. Dowdy," died a ripe scholar of seventy-four, the head of his profession.

Morison may have been carried away because he was so close to Channing and wrote so soon after his death. Channing's History, however, was indeed an impressive work. Apparently few read it anymore, and the publisher allowed it to go out of print some years ago. But there is still much to be learned from the Great Work.

Channing's preface in Volume I, published in 1905, told a great deal about what the finished product was to become. He intended to treat the growth of the nation as one continuous development, he announced, "from the political, military, institutional, industrial and social points of view." Channing's belief in progress, doubtless influenced by the evolutionary climate of opinion of his day, was made clear in what he called the "guiding idea" of his History: "to view the subject as the record of an evolution, and to trace the growth of the nation from the standpoint of that which preceded rather than from that which followed." He elaborated: "In other words, I have tried to see in the annals of the past the story of living forces, always struggling onward and upward toward that which is better and higher in human conception." Closely related to this "guiding idea" of evolutionary development was what Channing saw as "the most important single fact in our development," i.e., "the victory of the forces of union over those of particularism." This indeed was to provide a central theme for the Great Work. Finally, Channing knew that "the time and place of one's birth and breeding affect the judgment [of the historian], and the opportunity for error is frequent." He always tried, and urged others to try, to judge historical figures by the standards of their own time: "To estimate them by the conditions and ideas of the present day is to give a false picture," he said.

Channing took three volumes to reach 1789, three more to reach 1865. His third and sixth volumes were his best. Volume III was The American Revolution, 1761-1789, and volume VI The War for Southern Independence, actually covering all the way back to 1848. These two volumes are probably the outstanding ones of the series because Channing was at his best when he had a central theme, and especially when he was writing more traditional political-oriented history. He realized the importance of society, education, literature, etc., as he made clear even in his preface. But his efforts along these lines, for example in volume V where half the space is devoted to this kind of material, were not very successful, and seem somehow strangely unrelated to the over-all story.

"Commercialism, the desire for advantage and profit in trade and industry, was at the bottom of the struggle between England and America," wrote Channing in volume III, making it clear what his central theme for the Revolutionary period was. He had already placed himself clearly in the "Imperial School" of colonial historians in the preface, where he wrote that he "considered the colonies as parts of the English empire, as having sprung from that political fabric, and as having simply pursued a course of institutional evolution unlike that of the branch of the English race which remained behind in the old homeland across the Atlantic."

Placing Channing in any "school" of historians, however, is a tricky thing. Such a perceptive viewer of the course of American historical writing as Michael Kraus has had trouble with it. In a 1937 book, he placed Channing in a chapter on the Imperial School; but in a 1953 revision of the work, Channing is a part of "The Nationalist School." To complicate matters further, Kraus referred to Channing as "one of the earliest and finest products of the 'scientific school' of historiography in America," and in still another place vaguely mentioned "the school of Edward Channing," by which he apparently meant the problem-solving technique of historical research. However, there is really no contradiction here. On most aspects of colonial history, Channing aligned himself with the Imperial School; on the Civil War, he was one of the outstanding nationalists. And his scientific approach and problem-solving technique tie him to no particular school; indeed they serve to illustrate his independence and aloofness from all schools as such.

Though Channing's union over particularism theme obviously reached its peak in volume VI, there is not quite the coherence to this volume that there was to volume III. Nor is there something simple to explain the Civil War like "commercialism" did the Revolution. But if one makes the effort to piece his comments together, a pattern does emerge, and probably a much more realistic idea of how the war came about than can be gathered from historians who strive to prove one particular theory. It would go something like this: The war resulted from a natural, environmentally-produced sectionalism in which the two leading factors were slavery, economically and socially, and the view of the nature of the union, politically; and in the end, it became a purely emotional thing, for "The psychology of men's actions is often beyond the ken of the historian; but in this case sentiment overruled every other consideration in the North--and in the South." It is a shame that Channing did not live to complete his seventh volume, so that we would have his views on Reconstruction, those years following the war when sentiment continued to hold sway.

Time has passed Edward Channing's historical works by, and many of his methods. This should not be lamented. Channing himself knew it would happen. "No historian can hope to live as can a poet or an essayist," he once wrote, "because new facts will constantly rise to invalidate his most careful conclusions." Though some historians today could empathize with his aversion to cooperative series--"There are always a few good books in these publications and a lot of very poor ones" --the trend, already evident in Channing's day with the <u>American Nation Series</u> to which he contributed the Jefferson volume, will doubtless continue. Surely Channing's Great Work will be the last multi-volume study of all United States history by a single author. But of that small group of American historians, including Bancroft, McMaster, Rhodes, von Holst, and

Schouler, who wrote such works, Channing's bears the scrutiny of modern historical scholarship at least as well as any of them.

It is not easy to assess Channing's importance in American historiography. There is no doubt of the impact of such "thesis" historians as Beard and Turner. For a historian such as Channing, noted primarily for a comprehensive general history, determination of direct influence is much more difficult. Still, many of his students, including Samuel Eliot Morison, Evarts B. Greene, Carl Russell Fish, Samuel Flagg Bemis, and Howard K. Beale, have acknowledged their indebtedness to him. For his teaching, his bibliographical work, his textbooks, his meticulous historical methods, and literally hundreds of new insights into our history in his Great Work, Edward Channing deserves always to be remembered as a major figure in American historical writing.

EDWARD CHANNING AND THE NEGRO

In 1916, Edward Channing wrote a letter to J. Franklin Jameson which was clearly intended, at least partially, as a recommendation for Carter G. Woodson. "Woodson wrote his thesis under my guidance," Channing began.

> He impressed me as a very good man. He was more assertive than most of his race and was desirous of doing thorough work. He is accurate in details, but like most of us, white as well as black, sometimes overlooks an authority. I think you can trust him as fully as you can any colored man; but he has, of course, the defects of his color.[1]

The sixth volume of Channing's major work, <u>A History of the United States</u>, drew praise from one reviewer in 1925 for being so "convincing in. . . showing the mistake of the North in its belief that the negroid race is a gifted race."[2]

But, one must ask, are these two items really representative of Edward Channing's views of black Americans? Or, was he really as "bad" as these make him appear? The answer to both queries is no, not really.

Edward Channing was born in 1856 and died in 1931. He was the son of the poet Ellery Channing (1818-1901) and the great-nephew of William Ellery Channing (1780-1842), the founder of the American Unitarian movement. The Channings were related to many of the well-known families in Massachusetts and New England history, such as the Higginsons, Cabots, Lowells, and Emersons. As Edward Channing once wrote, he was "related more or less to all the 'Highnesses'."[3] But Channing early determined to make a contribution of his own, and his chosen field was history. He received a Ph.D. in that discipline from Harvard in 1880 and began his teaching career there in 1883. He remained at that institution for forty-seven years, finally retiring in 1929, just two years before his death.

There is a well-known story that Channing was once approached by a student who said, "My father wished me to inquire what relation you were to the great Channing."

Channing's response, delivered with a characteristic thump on the chest as he peered over his rimless glasses, was "I am the great Channing!"[4] Channing's students habitually referred to his major contribution, the six-volume History of the United States, as the "Great Work"--and so did he. Though this may appear a bit egotistical, it is certainly true that in the field of American historical writing, Edward Channing and his History are both thoroughly deserving of the label "great."

A complete list of Channing's writings is long and diverse, but his major contributions can be quickly delineated. The Jeffersonian System, 1801-1811 was published in 1906 as a volume in Albert Bushnell Hart's pioneering American Nation series. Channing wrote several textbooks, but by far his most significant was A Students' History of the United States, which went through five editions between 1898 and 1925. In the field of bibliography, Channing was responsible, along with Hart, for the ground-breaking 1897 Guide to the Study of American History; in 1912, Frederick Jackson Turner assisted in a revision of the Guide. This work was the predecessor of the indispensable Harvard Guide to American History of 1954, which was dedicated to Channing, Hart, and Turner.

Beyond a doubt Channing's most significant contribution was his "Great Work." It made him a member of that small group of American historians, including George Bancroft, John Bach McMaster, Hermann von Holst, James Ford Rhodes, and James Schouler, who produced multi-volume general histories of the United States. Channing's work was in six volumes, published between 1905 and 1925, covering from beginnings (1000) to 1865. Volume VI, dealing with the years 1848 to 1865, won the 1925 Pulitzer Prize. Channing came nearer to covering the entire span of American history than any of the authors of multi-volume general works, and he did so in a fashion which bears the scrutiny of modern historical scholarship at least as well as any of them. As Samuel Eliot Morison noted, "Channing accomplished what no man had done before, and what is not likely to be done again . . . with his own hand, and from his own research, he wrote a great history of the United States from the beginning of colonization to the close of the Civil War."[5]

Channing's importance in American historiography is difficult to assess. He was noted for no central thesis, such as the economic interpretation of Charles A. Beard or the frontier theory of Turner. This lack of controversy doubtless helps to account for the lack of attention to Channing in some quarters. Such a noted historian as Crane Brinton has recently stated that he feels Channing and his work are greatly underrated these days. [6] For his teaching, his bibliographical work, his textbooks, his meticulous historical methods, and literally hundreds of new insights into our history in his "Great Work," Edward Channing deserves still, as one scholar noted some twenty-five years ago, to be remembered as "one of the giants of American historical writing." [7]

The subject here, however, is Edward Channing and the Negro. It is to Channing's History that we must turn for most of his comments on that subject.

Gerald N. Grob and George Athan Billias, in the most recent edition of their well-known collection, Interpretations of American History, place Channing among the leading exponents of the "nationalist school" of historians on the Civil War, along with James Ford Rhodes and Woodrow Wilson. Some of the major characteristics of this school are: the beginning of a more balanced, less partisan picture of the Civil War; the belief that the war was an "irrepressible" conflict; and approval of the outcome of the war and subsequent developments such as the growth of industry and the Negro's being forced to accept a subordinate role in American life. [8]

Certainly Channing wrote in such a way in his sixth volume as to justify the "irrepressible conflict" label:

> By the middle of the [nineteenth] century, two
> distinct social organizations had developed
> within the United States, the one in the South and
> the other in the North. Southern society was
> based on the production of staple agricultural
> crops by slave labor. Northern society was
> bottomed on varied employments--agricultural,
> mechanical, and commercial--all carried on
> under the wage system. Two such divergent
> forms of society could not continue indefinitely
> to live side by side within the walls of one

government, even within the walls of so loosely constructed a system as that of the United States under the Constitution. One or the other of these societies must perish, or both must secure complete equality. . .or the two societies must separate absolutely and live each by itself under its own government. [9]

Some of Channing's treatment of the Negro in his "Great Work" tends to support Grob and Billias' contention about race as well. The first mention, however, in volume one, The Planting of a Nation in the New World, 1000-1660, is an interesting one, in which Channing points out the hypocrisy of slave-traders ordering their crews "to serve God daily" and "to love one another" and giving their ships such names as "The Jesus." "Of all the contradictions of history one that impresses the student is the constant and sincere religious fervor of the men with whom he comes into contact whose actions otherwise are often not commendable according to present day rules of conduct," Channing observed. But, he warned, "The standards of those days were not the standards of our day," then concluded hopefully, "and the standards of three hundred years hence will doubtless be unlike those of our time."[10]

In volume two, A Century of Colonial History, 1660-1760, Channing deals at some length with slavery for the first time, in a chapter on "Systems of Labor." Two things are of special note. Channing praised William Byrd as one of the "more far-sighted" of the Virginia planters who "lamented the increase of slavery" in that colony.[11] But, after a brief account of the 1712 and 1741 problems in New York that led to burnings, hanging, and deportation of blacks, he concluded:

> The condition of panic which was responsible for the cruel executions that have just been noted was undoubtedly due to the fact that there was not effective supervision of the black population in New York. In the southern colonies the plantation system with its attendant overseers and slave drivers made for an efficient condition of discipline. [12]

As Channing moved into the Revolutionary era with his third volume, he was able to discern the contradiction between the

49

ideals of liberty and equality and the continuation of slavery.
Neither white servitude nor black slavery ceased with the
Declaration of Independence, he noted. "The former was clearly
opposed to the doctrines formulated in that instrument and dis--
appeared within a generation; the latter, through economic
causes, became intensified in one section of the country."[13]
Channing insisted, however, that, by the end of the Revolution,

> Unquestionably, the leaders of public opinion in
> America were becoming restive on the subject of
> negro slavery. The slave owners themselves
> accounted for the inconsistency of their views as
> to human rights and holding blacks in bondage by
> saying that slaves were not members of the
> political society; but some of them had grave
> doubts as to the rightfulness of their own actions.[14]

Both Washington and Jefferson are among those cited as
examples. Certainly, asserted Channing, "The colonists in
general were bitterly hostile to the importation of negroes."
On that point, however, he footnoted the then-recent work of
W. E. B. DuBois on the "Suppression of the African Slave-
trade to the United States of America," and admitted that
"Presumably he [i. e., DuBois] would think that the statement
in the text is too strong."[15]

Channing's fourth volume, Federalists and Republicans,
1789-1815, includes no significant treatment of blacks or slavery.
Logically, the heart of his analysis of those subjects is to be
found in his fifth and sixth volumes, dealing collectively with
the period from the end of the War of 1812 to the end of the
Civil War.

A long chapter in volume five entitled "The Plantation
System and Abolitionism" is crucial. Channing gave a rather
critical evaluation of the radical abolitionists, but praised the
work of such moderates as John Quincy Adams and his own
great-uncle, William Ellery Channing, who, said Channing,
"trod the middle path that satisfied no one, but sometimes is
the path of wisdom."[16]

The plantation system itself appeared most unappealing to
the twentieth century New England historian. "The life on one

of these great plantations must have been monotonous in the extreme," he wrote.

> It was one ceaseless round of looking after the
> slaves, keeping them in health, seeing that they
> did not steal or run away, and superintending
> the superintendents or overseers . . . . All in
> all, the troubles and vexations of plantation
> life must have detracted immensely from the
> pleasures of existence and to this must be
> added the burden of debt that often hung over
> the owner of thousands of acres and hundreds
> of slaves. In fact, the great planter of the
> Cotton Belt had all the business cares of the
> prosperous Northern manufacturer or man
> of commerce with a multitude of petty human
> details thrown in. It is by no means improbable,
> as one Southern writer had intimated, that the slaves
> were often happier than their masters. [17]

Yet, note these interesting and revealing observations from Channing on slavery and race:

> The persistent and ever increasing demand
> for cotton fibre, the improvement of the cotton-
> gin, and the discovery that the short staple,
> green seed cotton plant throve marvelously
> in the uplands of South Carolina and Georgia
> and in the black belt to the westward, changed
> the whole course of economic and social
> existence in the South, and, indeed, governed
> the course of history of the United States down
> to the year 1865. In so far as Eli Whitney's
> perfection of the cotton-gin contributed to the
> cultivation of the upland cotton plant on a great
> scale it was a curse to the South, to the United
> States, and to humanity. [18]

Only a few pages later, Channing conceded that the "propensity of negroes to run away" was a "constant cause of anxiety" for slave owners, and suggested that this propensity was sometimes "the result of an inborn desire for freedom, especially on the part of those slaves who had a large admixture

51

of white blood in their veins."[19]   He speculated further on mis-
cegenation:

> From time to time it is not unusual for men to
> argue that the white race and the black race are
> different and that they are incapable of amal-
> gamation. This may all be true as to the
> ultimate merging of the two races, but mis-
> cegenation was common in the Slave States
> before 1861, although it may be going too far
> to assert that it was a distinct menace to the
> integrity of the white race.[20]

Finally, Channing's sixth, Pulitzer Prize-winning volume on
the Civil War era obviously includes much of relevance to us
here. But there is really no need to review everything he said
on slavery, its expansion into the territories, and the Civil War
itself. Rather, let us note two comments on slavery and one on
the Negro.

Channing strove visibly to be objective in analyzing the
institution of slavery. He noted that, because of their great
value, no planter was likely to work or punish his slaves to
excess. But he also admitted that there were valid objections
to slavery, and recounted a story attributed to Andrew Carnegie
which he felt exhibited "the essence of the objection to the
system."

> An Ohio judge is represented as interrogating a
> fugitive slave and upon the colored man telling
> him that he had plenty of food, good shelter,
> plenty of clothes, and a good master and that he
> did not have to work very hard, the white man
> suddenly asked, why if he had all these things
> did he run away, and the fugitive replied that
> the place he had left was open, that the judge
> could go down and take it, --and resumed his
> line of march for Canada.[21]

"Like everything else," concluded Channing, "the goodness or
the badness of the system depended upon the point of view."[22]

Channing addressed himself briefly to the oft-disputed

question of the profitability of slavery, concluding that before the great increase in slave prices after 1850, "it was probably true that on the best conducted plantations the slave gang was the cheapest and most efficient agricultural labor in the world in terms of the crop produced." Even after 1850, he concluded, "more slaves not more land was the need of the South."[23]

When he turned from the institution of slavery to the Negro himself, Channing was not quite so successful in remaining objective. "In his pure condition, undiluted by white or yellow blood, the negro is essentially a communist and a fatalist," wrote Channing.

> All treatments of Southern life by Northern writers gave an entirely false assessment of the weaknesses and the strengths of the slave system. They uniformly applied white standards to black life without any comprehension of the actualities of negroid, racial development. This was partly due to the inability of every man and woman to see good in unaccustomed ways of living of other persons; but it was more especially due to the fact that in those days knowledge of negroid institutions and conceptions of negroid ideals were very vague and extremely inaccurate. Since 1890, many competent explorers have visited Central Africa and the Congo and have set down in print the results of their observations and of their communings with the natives. Reading these many accounts, weighing them, and trying to draw judgment from them, it appears that it is about as hard for the Ethiop to change his institutional and racial conceptions as it is for him to alter the color of his skin. Both his institutions and his skin are matters of heredity. They have come down from a very remote past and are, even today, being handed on unchanged to future generations.[24]

It would, of course, have been very interesting to see what Channing had to say about the Negro after freedom. His seventh volume, however, which was virtually complete at the time of his death in 1931, was not only never published, but was destroyed. Thus, anything he said about the Negro in Reconstruction, for example, must be gleaned from his various textbooks, and is so brief and shallow in comparison to the material in his "Great Work" as to be virtually useless here.

What, then, can we say, in conclusion, of Edward Channing and the Negro? That he was a racist? Grob and Billias write of the nationalist historians:

> The climate of opinion around the turn of the century was such that few took occasion to protest the fact that blacks had not yet achieved a measure of equality with whites. Like most white Americans, many of these scholars--though by no means all--believed blacks to be inferior beings. Such a belief seemed to them to be buttressed by contemporary scientific findings. They therefore accepted the subordinate role of blacks in American society as a natural development. [25]

Channing included? Perhaps.

One of Channing's grandsons has emphasized his closeness with Thomas Wentworth Higginson--they were relatives and wrote a book together in 1893 entitled English History for American Readers--and suggested that "Colonel Higginson's influence must have been felt by Channing" in the area of race. [26] Again, perhaps so, but that influence must have done no more than to moderate Channing's views somewhat. Certainly there is no evidence to suggest that Channing was the egalitarian that the abolitionist, feminist, anti-imperialist, Colonel of the Black Regiment Higginson was. [27]

Based on the evidence briefly presented here, most of us, with the advantage of a 1979 perspective, would indeed consider Edward Channing a racist. But we should be careful, as Channing himself always tried to be, not to judge by the standards of our own day. Like everyone else, Channing was the product, his attitudes toward blacks were the product, of his time, place, race--his climate of opinion. In short, I think you can trust him as fully as you can any white historian of the early twentieth century; but he has, of course, the defects of his color--and his time.

NOTES

[1] Edward Channing to J. Franklin Jameson, June 1, 1816 [sic], John Franklin Jameson Collection, Manuscript Division, Library of Congress, Washington, D.C.

[2] C.M. Morrison, New York Evening Post Literary Review, September 5, 1925.

[3] Edward Channing, "Recollections of a Hitherto Truthful Man," p. 2. (This is an incomplete, unpublished autobiography written by Channing in 1929-1930. It is in the possession of his daughter, Mrs. Willard P. Fuller, of Chatham, Massachusetts. Her son, Willard P. Fuller, Jr., of San Andreas, California, edited and privately printed a limited number of copies of this work in 1967. The author wishes to thank these members of the Channing family for permission to use both versions of the work.)

[4] Samuel Eliot Morison, "Edward Channing: A Memoir," Proceedings of the Massachusetts Historical Society, LXIV (October, 1930-June, 1932), p. 252.

[5] Ibid., p. 284.

[6] Letter to the author from Crane Brinton, July 3, 1967.

[7] John A. DeNovo, "Edward Channing's 'Great Work' Twenty Years After," Mississippi Valley Historical Review, XXXIX (September, 1952), p. 257.
The present writer has made one brief effort and one longer one to assess Channing and his work. See: Davis D. Joyce, "American Historian: Edward Channing, 1856-1931," Historical Musings, II (Summer, 1974), pp. 60-64; and Davis D. Joyce, Edward Channing and the Great Work (The Hague: Nijhoff, 1974).

[8] Gerald N. Grob and George Athan Billias, Editors, Interpretations of American History: Patterns and Perspectives: Volume I: To 1877 (Third Edition; New York: The Free Press, 1978), pp. 366-368.

[9] Edward Channing, A History of the United States. Volume VI: The War for Southern Independence (New York: The Macmillan Company, 1925), pp. 3-4.

[10] Edward Channing, A History of the United States. Volume I: The Planting of a Nation in the New World, 1000-1660 (New York: The Macmillan Company, 1905), pp. 116-117.

[11] Edward Channing, A History of the United States. Volume II: A Century of Colonial History, 1660-1760 (New York: The Macmillan Company, 1908), p. 377.

[12] Ibid., p. 389.

[13] Edward Channing, A History of the United States. Volume III: The American Revolution, 1761-1789 (New York: The Macmillan Company, 1912), p. 553.

[14] Ibid., p. 556.

[15] Ibid., p. 557.

[16] Edward Channing, A History of the United States. Volume V: The Period of Transition, 1815-1848 (New York: The Macmillan Company, 1921), p. 170.

[17] Ibid., pp. 123-125.

[18] Ibid., p. 121.

[19] Ibid., p. 125.

[20] Ibid., pp. 127-128.

[21] Channing, History, vol. VI, p. 15.

[22] Ibid.

[23] Ibid., pp. 23 and 16.

[24] Ibid., pp. 19-20.

[25] Grob and Billias, p. 368.

[26] Letter to the author from Willard P. Fuller, Jr., February 22, 1979.

[27] The title is from probably the best book on Higginson, Howard N. Meyer, Colonel of the Black Regiment: The Life of Thomas Wentworth Higginson (New York: W.W. Norton and Company, Incorporated, 1967).

III

HISTORIOGRAPHY:

BOOK REVIEWS

Book reviewing is a rather thankless task for the historian, but a necessary one. It is also a skill which should be developed by students of history--and of other disciplines, for thinking critically about what one reads is a vital part of the educational process.

Presented here are reviews of several books in the general field of historiography. The first book reviewed is a collection of different views on a subject, the second a biography of a historian, and the other three all in various ways treat historiography and philosophy of history. (Pardon the use of the same supposedly clever line about available reading in the latter field in two of the reviews. Note that the reviews appeared in different journals, which also accounts for differences in form and style.)

American Negro Slavery: A Modern Reader, EDITED BY
ALLEN WEINSTEIN AND FRANK OTTO GATELL. New York:
Oxford University Press, 1973, 439 pages, Cloth, $9.50;
paper, $2.95.

There are too many edited historical works published today;
some of them seem to serve little purpose other than padding
the publication lists of the editors. Allen Weinstein and Frank
Otto Gatell have certainly done their share of editing. In
addition to the work under review, they have published The
Segregation Era, 1863-1954: A Modern Reader; American
Politics: A Modern Reader, and Readings in American Political History. But there is a difference: when Weinstein and
Gatell edit something, they really make a contribution.

The selections in this anthology are well-chosen, the brief
notes before each selection are helpful, the general introduction
is excellent, and the 30-page bibliography is, quite simply,
one of the best available. Here are the contents, with the
asterisks indicating selections that are new to this revised
edition :

Part I: THE ORIGIN

 *Winthrop D. Jordan, " 'Unthinking Decision': The
  Enslavement of Negroes in America to 1700 "
 David Brion Davis, "The Evolution of Slavery in British
  America and Latin America: A Comparison"

Part II: THE SLAVE

 Ulrich B. Phillips, "Southern Negro Slavery: A Benign
  View"
 Kenneth M. Stampp, "Southern Negro Slavery: 'To Make
  Them Stand in Fear' "
 *Stanley M. Elkins, "Slavery and Negro Personality"
 *George M. Fredrickson and Christopher Lasch,
  "Resistance to Slavery"
 *Sterling Stuckey, "Through the Prism of Folklore: The
  Black Ethos in Slavery"
 *Lawrence W. Levine, "Slave Songs and Slave Conscious-
  ness"
 *Eugene D. Genovese, "American Slaves and Their History"

Part III: THE MASTER

*William W. Freehling, "The Founding Fathers and
    Slavery"
*George M. Fredrickson, "Slavery and Race: The South-
    ern Dilemma"
John Hope Franklin, "The Militant South"
Eugene D. Genovese, "The Slave South: An Interpretation"

Part IV: THE SYSTEM

*David Brion Davis, "Slavery: A Comparative Approach"
Harold D. Woodman, "The Profitability of Slavery"
Robert S. Starobin, "Race Relations in Old South
    Industries"
Richard C. Wade, "Slavery in the Southern Cities"
*Carl N. Degler, "Slavery in Brazil and the United States:
    A Comparison"
*Emory M. Thomas, "Black Confederates: Slavery and
    Wartime"

Part V: ASSESSMENTS

Stanley M. Elkins, "On Eugene D. Genovese's The Poli-
    tical Economy of Slavery"
M.I. Finley, "On David Brion Davis's The Problem of
    Slavery in Western Culture"
*J.H. Plumb, "On Wintrhop D. Jordan's White Over
    Black: American Attitudes Toward the Negro,
    1550-1812"

Notice that 12 of the 22 selections are new. (Actually,
there was an excerpt from Jordan in Part I of the first edition,
but it was a different selection.) This is evidence, among
other things, of the vitality of the field, for the first edition
was published only five years ago. Indeed, this is one of the
major reasons an anthology like this is so valuable. Teachers
of history at all levels simply cannot keep up with all the
reading, especially in an area as prolific as black history in
recent years. If short-cuts must be taken, anthologies such
as this provide a helpful way to do it.

One must strain to come up with meaningful criticism of

this book. It does seem unfair, since we have Elkins on
Genovese, that we do not have Genovese on Elkins, as we did
in the first edition. But Genovese is well represented, and
too many additional selections would have made the length
unreasonable. (This edition is 439 pages, compared to the
first edition's 366.) And it seems a shame that there was not
time to include a selection from one of the two very recent
books which represent excellent efforts to view slavery from the
slave's perspective: George P. Rawick's From Sundown to
Sunup: The Making of the Black Community and John W.
Blassingame's The Slave Community: Plantation Life in the
Ante-Bellum South.

"Slavery's central importance to the national experience
from Jamestown to Appomattox (and beyond) remains the
essential thread linking together the two dozen selections,"
write the editors in their preface. And their work gets very
close to providing the "balanced, one-volume coverage of
North American slavery's 240 year history" that they hope it
will. The Library Journal called the first edition an "excellent
anthology." It still is--only more so.

The Life of John Lothrop Motley, by J. Guberman. Martinus Nijhoff, The Hague, 1973. 155 pp.

By Guberman's own admission in his preface, it is primarily as a historian that Motley deserves to be remembered. Yet only about twelve to fifteen pages in this book of 155 are devoted to his historical works, The Rise of the Dutch Republic, History of the United Netherlands, and The Life and Death of John of Barneveld, Advocate of Holland. Dealt with at great length are the more personal aspects of Motley's life, like his relationship with "his two closest friends, " Otto von Bismarck and Oliver Wendell Holmes, and, especially, his diplomatic career, of which more later.

This obvious imbalance is only the most important of many flaws in Guberman's book. There is no index; there are no footnotes; and the bibliography is about half a page in length. There are errors and inconsistencies of punctuation, capitalization, and spelling which are irritating. (It is bad enough to have to read "succession" for "secession" in a student's essay; one should not have to tolerate it in a book.) There are far too many lengthy quotations--one extreme example is a Hamilton Fish letter dealing with Motley's dismissal as American ambassador to Great Britain which covers pages 127 through 142! Besides that, quotations are not handled correctly, since none of the excessively large number of of excessively long quotations are indented. Finally, there are many cases where Guberman's conclusions simply do not grow logically out of the evidence he has presented. One example of this, perhaps a minor one, is to be found in the first paragraph of the book. After admitting that Motley and his father held "quite opposite principles, " had never been able to communicate with each other, and that only one or two letters to his father were to be found in Motley's entire correspondence, Guberman concludes: "There can be no doubt, however, they both had a warm affection for each other. " No footnote--there are none, remember? And the scanty evidence Guberman has presented on the subject tends to contradict his conclusion.

Motley's diplomatic career, emphasized more than any-thing else in this book, serves as a more important example of both the quotation problem and the failure to draw conclusions consistent with the evidence. Suffice it to say that the long series of letters thrown together in chapter thirteen almost without comment by Guberman does not necessarily lead directly to the conclusion of the preface that Motley "was degraded from his post as an Ambassador to the Court of Saint James, for the most frivolous and malicious of reasons, and condemned to an existence of unhappiness and loneliness during the remaining years left to him, as the reward for faithful and conscientious service to his country." (That this was Motley's second such removal, following a similar one from his post in Austria a few years earlier, raises some questions also, although they are unanswered here.)

Despite all its weaknesses, this is an interesting and informative book. One gets the impression that there is need for a good book on Motley, and most of the material for writing it is here--but this is not the book.

Historians and the Living Past: The Theory and Practice of
Historical Study, by Allan J. Lichtman and Valerie French.
Arlington Heights, Illinois: AHM Publishing Corporation,
1978. 267 pages. $5.95, paper.

"We are convinced that history illumines the world as
brightly as any field of study, yet current enrollment trends
suggest that too few students share our view of history's value
and excitement," write Lichtman and French in their preface.
They have taught a course at the American University entitled
"Historians and the Living Past," from which this book is an
outgrowth. Here they have tried to communicate "not only the
how and why of historical study and our enthusiasm for our
own special fields (the recent United States and classical anti-
quity), but also the intellectual excitement found in the whole
historical enterprise."

Sometimes they succeed; sometimes they don't. The book
explores five major aspects of historical study. First, two
chapters explore "questions relating to the procedures and
methods used by historians to comprehend past experience."
Second, one chapter is devoted to the general approaches mankind has used to explain the past, i.e., myth, force, and man.
Third and fourth, some recent developments in historical
study are covered, and family and local history are discussed
as ways history can bring people closer to their personal
heritage.

What Lichtman and French really do in these four parts
is to move from philosophy of history (i.e., though about
history) into historiography (i.e., the history of history).
Anyone who has tried to introduce undergraduates to the
philosophy of history knows how difficult it can be; most
reading in the field is a sure cure for insomnia. Lichtman
and French don't do much better, though perhaps this is not so
much a criticism of them as it is a comment on the inherent
difficulty of making cause and effect, generalization, covering
laws, etc., interesting and understandable to the average
student. On historiography, the authors do much better,
especially as they move into some of the more recent fields
such as psychohistory and quantification.

The fifth major aspect of historical study explored is

historical research and writing. This part is very good, with the one possible criticism being that Lichtman and French don't go into such mundane matters as how to do a footnote, bibliographical reference, etc., so that use of some work that does might be necessary in conjunction with this one.

Actually, though Lichtman and French don't say so, there is a sixth part to the book. It comes in the first chapter, "Past and Present: History and Contemporary Analysis," and is an effort to demonstrate "one of the fundamental premises of this book: what we believe about the past powerfully influences our perceptions of the present and decisions about the future." Through an examination of a newspaper column by George F. Will on the Nixon pardon and George Kennan's American Diplomacy, Lichtman and French do an excellent job of illustrating their arguments about history's relevance: "The past provides our only source of information for evaluating current affairs and making predictions about the future.... Without such knowledge we would be as bewildered as a quarterback entering the fourth quarter of a football game without knowing the score, the amount of elapsed time, or the successes and failures of plays and players."

John T. Marcus. Sub Specie Historiae: Essays in the Manifestation of Historical and Moral Consciousness. Cranbury, New Jersey: Associated University Presses, 1980. Pp. 325. Cloth, $22.50.

I knew when I had to look the title of this book up in the glossary that I was in for a difficult task reading and reviewing it. ("Sub specie historiae" means, according to Marcus, "from the perspective of historical-mindedness.")

The book review editor expressed concern to me that the book might be too "arcane" for the pages of Teaching History. I had to look that up too, in the dictionary: I decided it was not. The editor's concern continued: "This book is somewhat unusual compared with our usual review volumes, most of which are potential classroom materials. I want to broaden our scope to discuss books that deal with the philosophy of history and of pedagogy, and this appears to do that." Indeed it does, not with pedagogy but with the philosophy of history. And I support the idea of broadening the scope of reviews in Teaching History to include such works.

The problem with Sub Specie Historiae, most simply stated, is that it is an extremely difficult book. This is doubtless partially due to the very nature of philosophy of history. Anyone who has tried to introduce students to the field knows that most available reading is a sure cure for insomnia. This book, if it is for students at all, is only for the most advanced graduate students. Basically, it is probably intended for teachers in the field who can hopefully pass the insights gleaned from it--and there certainly are some--on to their students in more practical form.

One problem with the book is that it consists of a series of essays written over a long period of time, not always clearly related to each other, and with considerable over-lapping and choppiness resulting. The central theme of the book, for example, is stated several times; nowhere is it stated more succinctly than on page 293: "the role of historical understanding in a redefinition of moral judgement." More of that central theme is made clear, as is the difficulty of the language, in this passage from page 296:

Suffice it for me to note here that my formulation of
man's highest wordly historical responsibility
as the perpetuation of moral sensibility constitutes
a fulfillment of the entelechal mode, and hence a
repudiation of nihilism, without teleology. It
presents an ongoing task and future-directed
concern, informed by critical understanding of man's
past experience, that goes beyond both radical
relativism and historical nominalism. At the same
time, it transcends the realm of mystique-feeling
and its absolutized historical objectives, with their
implicitly totalitarian salvation.

Sub Specie Historiae is divided into two "books," the first
consisting of a comparative analysis of Western, Chinese, and
Indian concepts of historicity. Interestingly, an article in the
June, 1980, issue of The American Historical Review by George
Macklin Wilson does much the same thing for Japan ("Time and
History in Japan"). The second book, on the other hand, is a
view of western historical thought from within. The theme
underlying both is that Western civilization is so history-
oriented that the recovery of a sense of purpose in the study
of history has a direct bearing on Western intellectual and
moral life, and on the prospect of reestablishing some values
once held in common.

In short, Sub Specie Historiae is a book that unfortunately
limits its potential value by phrasing most of its insights in
such unaccustomed language that most readers won't get
them; indeed, most who begin the book probably won't finish
it. Perhaps one can make a case that anything worth
saying is worth saying in a fashion readilty understandable to
some significant audience. And surely one can insist that
any book that attempts to convince someone that history is
valuable, clearly part of Marcus's intent, to be successful
must at the very least say so in reasonably intelligible
language.

Irony and Consciousness: American Historiography and Reinhold Niebuhr's Vision, by Richard Reinitz. Lewisburg, Pennsylvania: Bucknell University Press, 1980. 230 pages. $19.50, cloth.

This book probably makes a greater contribution to our understanding of American history than Reinhold Niebuhr's The Irony of American History, which inspired it.

Reinitz accepts Niebuhr's definition of irony, as somewhat refined by Gene Wise (American Historical Explanations: A Strategy for Grounded Inquiry), and he even chooses to refer to it as "Niebuhrian (or humane) irony:" "We perceive a human action as ironic . . . when we see the consequences of that action as contrary to the original intention of the actor and can locate a significant part of the reason for the discrepancy in the actor himself or in his intention." (p. 19) Irony thus defined must be carefully distinguished from other forms of irony (rhetorical irony, the irony of fate, romantic irony) and from such related concepts as paradox, pathos, and tragedy, insists Reinitz.

The central argument of the book is stated clearly in the preface:

> the growth in the use of Niebuhrian irony in American historical writing is an indication of a maturation of American historical consciousness and is representative of the development of a more critical attitude toward our past. The writing of American history, like American culture in general, has been afflicted with exaggerated conceptions of American innocence, virtue, wisdom, and power, and with the pretension to chosenness. The movement of the use of Niebuhrian irony from the periphery to the center of our perceptions of our past is an indication of the diminution of such illusions and myths.

To support his argument, Reinitz devotes the major portion of his book to an exmination of irony in the work of several American historians--after establishing the approach through a summary of Niebuhr's work and a brief look at irony in European history. These case studies are the strongest part of the book; very difficult material conceptually is clarified somewhat by showing how it really operates in specific historian's works. Among the earlier historians examined are Francis Parkman, Richard Hildreth, Henry Adams, and Carl Becker. But the extensive treatment is given to the three major post-World War II consensus historians: Richard Hofstadter, Daniel Boorstin, and Louis Hartz.

Interestingly, Reinitz is at pains to disprove the notion that irony is an attitude with conservative, or at least anti-radical, implications: "It is perhaps incompatible with programmatic radicalism but it is a radical tool insofar as it can expose the illusions that perpetuate the contradictions of American life." (p. 26) Yet, as noted, his major examples of the use of an ironic interpretation of American history come from consensus historians. Reinitz knew better than to force these writers into a narrow mold, however, and he knew that while they might see consensus in our history they did not, with the exception of Boorstin, necessarily like it. Hofstadter's chapter on Lincoln in The American Political Tradition he considered "one of the finest examples of Niebuhrian irony in American historical writing," (p. 144) while Boorstin's "conservative" and "apologetic" work shows him to be "too committed to our virtues and our uniqueness to have the distance required for irony." (p. 160)

Richard Reinitz edited a useful volume in 1970 entitled Tensions in American Puritanism, his only book before his untimely death in the fall of 1979. Fortunately, this volume was ready for publication; it is too bad that we will never have the "general interpretation of American history based upon his work on irony" that the dust jacket informs us he was working on at the time of his death.

Why the claim that Reinitz perhaps made more of a contribution with Irony and Consciousness than Niebuhr himself with The Irony of American History? Niebuhr, you see, wrote in 1952. His religious views, his demonic perception of communism--in short, his being a product of the Cold War atmosphere--limited him somewhat. He developed a

73

brilliant concept, but failed to apply it adequately. Said Reinitz: "That it was Niebuhr's neoorthodox Christianity that led him to the idea of ironic history and also in part interfered with his ability to write such history effectively is in itself a nice illustration of Niebuhrian irony." (p. 34) Reinitz, on the other hand, thanks to the passage of time, his own obviously brilliant mind, and the case study method he utilized so effectively, was able to give good support to his concluding claim that irony is "peculiarly suited to our situation; it is the perception of our past most compatible with our deepest understanding of historical complexity and the most useful in the present in our effort to free ourselves from the burden of those illusions, rooted in the past, which continue to lead us to act so as to contradict our own best intentions." (p. 183)

What of this book's potential for classroom use? Despite Reinitz's abilities, this is still a difficult book suitable for graduate students and perhaps the most advanced undergraduates. It would be a good idea to have students read the works of the historians discussed in Reinitz in conjunction with reading Reinitz.

IV

INNOVATIVE APPROACHES TO HISTORY

One of the responses to the crisis of history in recent years has been the development of innovative approaches, in teaching the old courses as well as in developing new ones. Experiments in History Teaching is a valuable collection of reports on such experiences published by the Harvard-Danforth Center for Teaching and Learning in 1977. The items in this section grow out of two of my own experimental courses in recent years.

An earlier version of the article on understanding history through science fiction was presented as a paper at the Missouri Valley History Conference in 1977.

I did a slightly revised version of the "Revising History with Ecology" course in January of 1978, and a significantly revised and expanded version in a full semester format in the fall of that year under the title "American Environmental History." A valuable textbook which was new at that time was added to the reading: American Environmental History: The Exploitation and Conservation of Natural Resources, by Joseph M. Petulla.

The article on Albert B. Fall grew out of my M.A. thesis, completed in the early 1960's; it went through drastic revision in view of my heightened consciousness resulting from the ecological crusade and my teaching of the courses in environmental history. It was presented as a paper to the 1979 meeting of the Oklahoma Association of College History Professors; somehow it seems even more relevant now in terms of the stance of Secretary of the Interior James Watt.

(Any differences in footnote style between the various essays in this collection reflect the requirements of the journals in which they appeared. They are left the way they appeared rather than made consistent here in order to illustrate different approaches; the preferred style is presented in the opening essay.)

THE PAST THROUGH TOMORROW:
UNDERSTANDING HISTORY THROUGH SCIENCE FICTION

The central character in Ward Moore's remarkable 1955
science fiction novel, Bring the Jubilee, is Hodgins McCormick
Backmaker, a historian. At one point in the story, he specu-
lates about the nature of history:

> I also began to understand the central mystery
> of historical theory. When and what and how and
> where, but the when is the least. Not chronology
> but relationship is ultimately what the historian
> deals in. The element of time, so vital at first
> glance, assumes a constantly more subordinate
> character. That the past is past becomes ever
> less important. Except for perspective it might
> as well be the present or the future or, if one
> can conceive it, a parallel time. I was not
> investigating a petrification but a fluid. Were it
> possible to know fully the what and how and where
> one might learn the why, and assuredly if one
> grasped the why he could place the when at will. [1]

More simply, as William Faulkner said it, "The past is never
dead; it is not even past. "[2]

Since I became involved in using science fiction to understand history, many people have insisted that it is a gimmick,
that there is little relationship between history, which deals
with the past, and science fiction, most of which deals with the
future. I draw again from American literature for a bit of
dialogue which helps to illustrate the contrary. "For God's
sake, forget the past," insists one character to another in
Eugene O'Neill's "Long Day's Journey into Night. " The response: "Why? How can I? The past is the present, isn't it?
It's the future, too. We all try to lie out of that but life won't
let us. "[3]

My basic point is that the past, the present, and the future
are all interrelated, part of a continuum. Thus, understanding
any one of them helps to understand the other two. A friend of
mine in history at Metropolitan State College in Denver has
drawn a cartoon to illustrate this. It shows a ship about to run

into an iceberg. Of course, only the tip of the iceberg is visible to the ship's captain. The tip is the present. Under the water is the massive portion of the iceberg--the past. The water itself is the future. The point is made visually and very effectively that if we do not realize that the past is a major part of the present, we face a very real risk of running aground on the present and never even knowing the future. "History repeats itself," as Thomas A. Bailey has written, "because no one was listening the first time."[4]

But what, you might ask, do bug-eyed monsters and space ships have to do with history? The answer, of course, is that much science fiction does deal with such topics, and while it justifies itself as escapism if nothing else, it really cannot be used all that productively to understand history. There is, however, a significant amount of science fiction, and apparently an increasing amount, that falls into one of three categories which I think can help us approach history.

The first is science fiction which involves alteration of historical events. Bring the Jubilee is an example; its setting is the United States after the loss of the "War of Southron Independence" to the Confederate States of America. The U.S. is a third-rate power in a world dominated by the Confederacy and the German Union, and the former Mexico City is now Leesburg. But the hero travels through time to a crucial turning point in the battle of Gettysburg because of his historian's curiosity. He accidentally gets caught up in the battle and causes it to come out differently--i.e., the way we know it really did come out! Another example is T.R. Fehrenbach's short story, "Remember the Alamo," in which an historian of the future, through time travel, arrives at the scene just on the eve of the Battle of the Alamo. Of course, he knows historically how the battle came out, but he gets involved in an advisory capacity and has an impact on the battle that makes it come out differently. And, just to show you how inside-out that version is,[5] "Remember the Alamo" becomes a Mexican rallying cry. Such "alternate history" science fiction can be used very productively to make us think of the impact if historical events had turned out differently and, therefore, the importance of them turning out the way they did.

The second category is science fiction which uses the past

80

and the present to project different possible futures. Harlan
Ellison, a master of this genre, which he is fond of calling
"speculative fiction," has edited an important anthology of such
stories under the title Dangerous Visions. [6] Ecological science
fiction provides an excellent example of this type of theme:
viewing the present state of the environment, and how it got this
way historically, science fiction writers have speculated in
many different ways about the possible ecological futures before
us. [7]

The third category is the broadest: it is science fiction
that simply treats subjects in a futuristic setting which are in
reality timeless. Indeed, such works need not necessarily even
be futuristic, as evidenced by Star Wars: the movie begins with
the words, "A long time ago, in a galaxy far, far away. . . ."
Laurence M. Janifer's novel, Power, is an excellent example of
this genre. It deals with a rebellion on board a space ship
belonging to Empire Earth in the far distant future. But the
document issued by the rebels is reminiscent of every great
document for human liberty in history; it speaks of concepts
like liberty, freedom, equality--ideas long since forgotten by
the leaders of Empire Earth. Also, the leader of the rebellion
is the son of one of the most powerful political figures in the
empire, and he has a brother who is a major figure in one of the
churches. [8] Through this science fiction novel, students can be
directed into a discussion of many questions. What is the nature of power? What motivates revolutionaries? Do revolu-
tions succeed? Has there always been a generation gap? What
is the role of religion in politics? What have concepts like
liberty, freedom, and equality meant historically? Does human
history show a movement away from them or toward them?

At the University of Tulsa, an undergraduate seminar program in the history department allows exploration of topics of
obvious interest and importance which are not dealt with, or at
least not adequately, within the framework of the regular
curriculum. The seminars are limited to 15 students. In the
fall of 1976, I offered "The Past Through Tomorrow: Understanding History Through Science Fiction."

Our "core" reading, which we began the semester by
discussing together, consisted of Transformations: Understand-

ing World History through Science Fiction and Transformations II: Understanding American History through Science Fiction, both edited by Daniel Roselle, and Political Science Fiction: An Introductory Reader, edited by Martin Harry Greenberg and Patricia S. Warrick.[9] Roselle's volumes consist of ten short stories each organized by historical topics and time periods. Greenberg and Warrick is an anthology also, organized around such political science topics as ideology and political philosophy, political leadership, elections and electoral behavior, political violence and revolution, diplomacy and international relations, and conflict resolution.

Growing out of this reading and discussion together, each student, in close consultation with me, selected a topic to pursue extensively for the rest of the semester and to report back on to the group at the end. These topics included war, urban science fiction, women in science fiction, ecological science fiction, the history of science fiction, science fiction of the past as history, social attitudes in science fiction, technology and changing life-styles, and such authors as Ray Bradbury, Issac Asimov, and R.A. Lafferty. I constantly insisted that the students be aware of the historical foundation of their topic; indeed, it was primarily at this point in the seminar that a significant amount of "pure" history was utilized in both reading and discussion. For example, on women in science fiction, I encouraged the student to ask such questions as whether the roles science fiction writers envision for women in the future are meaningfully related to women's roles today and especially historically; the same approach was used on ecological science fiction and most of the other topics as well. On each of the topics, especially those where the student involved showed any lack of mastery of the fundamental historical information, I suggested reading which would supply such information.

For another, smaller project, students selected a science fiction novel to read and discuss with the class which they felt was helpful for understanding history. By this time, most of the students had a reasonably firm grasp of what the course was all about, so the selection process was essentially an independent one. Choices varied greatly, and included Ray Bradbury's Fahrenheit 451 and Andre Norton's The Time Traders, a novel with a Cold War setting in which both Russians and Americans, through time travel, mine the past for technologies which will give them an advantage in the present.[10]

The seminar involved a blend of methods, including lecture, reading, reports, discussion, guest speakers (e.g., a member of our philosophy department with a presentation entitled "The Future: A Sketch of Possibilities"), and films (e.g., "Future Shock"). Also, a brief personal essay came due at the end of the semester to encourage each student to think about the content of the course in an over-all way.

Student essays and responses on a quantified evaluation form would indicate that the course was a remarkable success. The over-all rating was a 4.3 on a 5-point scale; nothing ranked lower than a 3.4 (Interestingly enough, that was "Future Shock," and the major reason, ironically, seemed to be that the film itself is so dated now!).[11] The seminar also provided an excellent example of a phenomenon unfortunately all too rare in the world of higher education--having fun while learning. And it offered an excellent way to capitalize on the current popularity of science fiction. Because of its flexibility, this idea could be adapted to every level from high school to continuing education, and to every format from seminars to interim terms to summer sessions to independent study.

On a cautionary note, with a topic of this type, as historians we must be careful to insist that we know better than to try to predict the future. For some reason not entirely clear to me, that has been a central criticism of my work in this area. I insist that I am simply using futuristic literature to provide a different and broader perspective on the present and the past. I remind the critics of these words of eminent historian, E.H. Carr: "Good historians, I suspect, whether they think about it or not, have the future in their bones. Besides the question: Why? the historian also asks the question: Whither?"[12] And I remind them of these meaningful comments of New Left historian Staughton Lynd about the nature of the historian's involvement with the future:

> What distinguishes the historian from other social
> scientists is not that he writes about the past but
> that he considers things in process of development.
> "History" and "sociology" are not concerned with
> different objects; they are different ways of looking

83

at the same object. Hence the historian need not
be embarrassed if he concerns himself more with
the present and future than with the past . . .
the historian's business with the future is not to
predict but to envision, to say (as Howard Zinn
has put it) not what will be but what can be. The
past is ransacked, not for its own sake, but as
a source of alternative models of what the future
might become.[13]

NOTES

[1] Ward Moore, Bring the Jubilee (New York, 1955), 137-138.

[2] Faulkner made the same point many different places. He
once said that "no man is himself, he is the sum of his past.
There is no such thing really as was because the past is. It is
a part of every man, every woman, and every moment."
Frederick L. Gwynn and Joseph L. Blotner, eds., Faulkner in
the University: Class Conferences at the University of Virginia,
1957-1958 (Charlottesville, 1959), 84.

[3] Eugene O'Neill, Long Day's Journey into Night (New
Haven, 1956), 87.

[4] Thomas A. Bailey, "The Mythmakers of American History," Journal of American History, LV (June, 1968), 20.

[5] The story is included in Daniel Roselle, ed., Transformations II: Understanding American History through Science
Fiction (Greenwich, Connecticut, 1974), 49-63.

[6] Harlan Ellison, ed., Dangerous Visions, 3 vols. (New
York, 1967-1969). The idea worked so well Ellison edited a
second, two-volume anthology, Again, Dangerous Visions
(New York, 1972-1973). Still another, The Last Dangerous
Visions, was promised, but apparently never published.

[7] Roger Elwood and Virginia Kidd, eds., The Wounded
Planet (New York, 1973), is one anthology of such fiction.

[8] Lawrence M. Janifer, Power (New York, 1974).

[9] Both volumes of Transformations were published by Fawcett, the first in 1973, the second in 1974. Unfortunately, both are already out of print, though copies are still available in some bookstores. Also, many of the stories are available in the works of individual authors. Political Science Fiction was published by Prentice-Hall in 1974, and is still available, as are similar collections in sociology and anthropology. Social Education is one of the few journals which have published in this field. Roselle's Transformations originally saw print as a special issue in February, 1973; "Teaching American History with Science Fiction" by Bernard C. Hollister appeared in February, 1975. It was basically bibliographical and focused on cultural shock and future shock, with a few suggestions on economics, urbanization, minorities, politics, international relations, and contemporary America.

[10] Others were Citizen of the Galaxy by Robert Heinlein; The Stainless Steel Rat Saves the World by Harry Harrison; Day after Tomorrow and Depression or Bust by Mack Reynolds; Brain Wave by Poul Anderson; Times without Number by John Brunner; Dune and Dune Messiah by Frank Herbert; Childhood's End by Arthur C. Clarke; and Andromeda Gun by John Boyd.

[11] The quantified evaluation form referred to was one designed specifically for the seminar. However, that semester the university was also using the "Student Instructional Report" of the Educational Testing Service. Among the interesting statistics, 92% agreed that the course "encouraged students to think for themselves," 75% that it "raised challenging questions or problems for discussion," and 100% that their interest in the subject area had been stimulated. The books used were rated satisfactory or better by 83% of the students, and the over-all value of the course satisfactory or better by 92% (50% excellent.)

[12] E.H. Carr, What is History? (New York, 1962), 143.

[13] Staughton Lynd, "Historical Past and Existential Present," in Theodore Roszak, ed., The Dissenting Academy (New York, 1967), 107.

REVISING HISTORY WITH ECOLOGY

In 1970, at the peak of the "ecology crusade" of the late 1960s and early 1970s, Wilbur R. Jacobs jarred the historical profession, or at least that segment of it interested in frontier history, with an article entitled "Frontiersmen, Fur Traders, and Other Varmints: An Ecological Appraisal of the Frontier in American History."[1] As evidenced by his title, the fur trade provided the focal point. Historians, he wrote, "have failed to impress their readers with the utterly destructive impact that the fur trade had upon the North American continent and the American Indian."[2] But the fur trade was just a part of the broader problem of what Jacobs called "the conquistador mentality that has so long dominated the writing of much American history." Jacobs pulled no punches in describing the problem:

> Until recently historians have largely ignored the ecological challenge. Yet truthful, interesting American history, double-barreled and difficult to write, is in part the revolting story of how we managed to commercialize all that we could harness and control with our technical skills. It is, in its unvarnished state, an unpleasant narrative of the reckless exploitation of minerals, waterways, soil, timber, wildlife, wilderness, and Indians, a part of a larger story of man's rape of nature over centuries.[3]

Jacobs, of course, knew better than to condemn our ancestors for what they did. "They acted in a manner consistent with their circumstances," he noted. "When the sky was darkened by thousands of pigeons, the normal, expected reaction was to kill them off wastefully."[4] What cannot be excused is the continuation of such attitudes into our own era of scarcity; the problem is perhaps not so much with our history as with historians. Finally, Jacobs ended on a hopeful note. "The movement to halt the destruction and pollution of the natural environment is now taking root all over the world," he said, and historians can contribute to the success of that movement, among other ways, "by zeroing in on the origins of the destruction of our environment."[5]

Jacobs' essay was one of the items Roderick Nash chose for

inclusion in his 1972 collection, Environment and Americans: The Problem of Priorities. I used that book in a freshman-level survey course in United States history in 1975-1976. I was pleasantly surprised at the exceptionally positive response of my students to the book, and especially to the kind of thinking embodied in Jacobs' article. Thus, I began to think of a way to capitalize in some formal academic fashion on that high level of interest. At the same time, admittedly, I would receive some satisfaction from feeling that I was contributing something legitimate in the academic realm to the environmental movement, which I had been interested and involved in personally for several years.

At the University of Tulsa, the greatest opportunity we have for innovation is the Interim Term. It is a four-week session squeezed into the month of January, between the two regular semesters. I proposed a course for the 1977 Interim Term entitled "Revising History with Ecology."[6] The course was described in the schedule as "a history of American attitudes toward the environment, their use and abuse of it, and the history of the conservation movement, including the contemporary ecology crusade." Even the positive response to Nash did not prepare me for how well the course went. From drawing power --the maximum class size of 25 was reached quite early in the enrollment period--to the final evaluation students made of the course--4.5 on a 5.0 scale--it was a remarkable success.

Students were expected to purchase and read two books which constituted the core reading. These were Douglas H. Strong, The Conservationists[7] and Roderick Nash, editor, The American Environment: Readings in the History of Conservation.[8] Strong's book is a brief, illustrated, imminently readable series of biographical sketches of those individuals most important in the history of the conservation movement, from such "forerunners" as Henry David Thoreau, through such giants as Gifford Pinchot and Aldo Leopold, to such modern disciples as Stewart Udall. Nash's book is entirely different; in his own words, it is "an inexpensive collection of readings illustrating the development of the American conservation movement in theory and practice."[9] Nash has done an excellent job of editing. His general introduction ("The Potential of Conservation History"), introductions to each section, and brief paragraphs introducing each selection are all excellent.

87

Selections run all the way from George Catlin's 1832 proposal for a national park to a 1973 interview with David Brower, founder of Friends of the Earth. Along the way, there are excerpts from the writings of all those dealt with by Strong, plus Rachel Carson, Barry Commoner, Ralph Nader, William O. Douglas, and many others. In short, both Strong and Nash are excellent books, and supplement each other very well.

Not much of the course consisted of lectures; I felt it should be as non-traditional mechanically as it was in terms of content. One way I attempted to accomplish this was through the use of a significant number of audio-visual aids, primarily films. Most of these were available from the local city-county library, some through our own university library, and in only two instances was it necessary to rent or purchase them from outside. One tape was used, "Native American Spiritual Values," in which Russell Means of the American Indian Movement insists that all Indians are natural-born ecologists. There was a total of nine films, including: "Once Upon A Wilderness," an excellent film which uses passages from an early pioneer's journal to impress upon the viewer that the attitudes of 150 years ago toward the environment are no longer appropriate; "Before the Mountain Was Moved," a moving documentary record of the efforts of a peoples' lobby to save the mountains of Raleigh County, West Virginia, from strip mining; "At the Crossroads: The Story of America's Endangered Species;" "Energy: The Nuclear Alternative," one part of a valuable four-part series on the energy crisis; and "Population and the American Future."

In addition to defining ecology,[10] and re-viewing American history from an ecological perspective, it was my belief that the course should involve the perspectives of other disciplines, since ecology is by its very nature an interdisciplinary concern. Thus, one crucial element of the course--and the element responded to most positively of all by the students--was a guest lecture series. The speakers were an anthropologist who talked about "Indians as Ecologists" (He differed with the thrust of the Russell Means tape.), a historian who has recently completed a book on the Tulsa District of the U.S. Army Corps of Engineers to talk on that work and examine the environmental image of the Corps, an economist with a presentation on "The Economics of Environmentalism," a physicist who used a computerized "energy-environment simulator" to explore the potential environmental impact of different types of energy utilization (He was, para-doxically, a Sierra Club member who supports nuclear energy.), a geographer with a presentation entitled "Land and Life: Ecology in Geography," a chemical engineer who discussed conservation of mineral resources, the chairman of the local chapter of the Sierra Club to discuss the important role of that organization in the conservation movement, and a botanist to talk on the perhaps central issue of "Population Ecology."[11]

In addition to the Strong and Nash books, each student was expected to select another book in the general area of environmental history for a book review, both oral and written. Selections ranged from Donald W. Whisenhunt's The Environment and the American Experience: A Historian Looks at the Ecological Crisis, Henry Nash Smith's Virgin Land: The American West as Symbol and Myth, and Roderick Nash's Wilderness and the American Mind, through Thoreau's Walden, Pinchot's Fight for Conservation, and Leopold's Sand County Almanac, to The Energy Balloon by Stewart Udall and others, and What Every Woman Should Know and Do About Pollution by Betty A. Ottinger.

Grades were based on attendance, participation, book review, and, finally, a personal essay at the end of the course (a "react paper") to attempt to wrap it all up and see what it meant. Students could elect to take the course either on a Pass-Fail basis or the traditional ABCDF scale; 75 percent chose the latter. The course met three hours a day, five days a week, for two weeks. (That's one thing I will change when I teach the course again; it was simply too little time to really do and absorb everything.)

Both the personal essays students wrote at the end of the course and the quantified evaluation forms which I designed specifically for the course indicated an overwhelmingly positive response. Typical comments included: "This class was probably the most worthwhile I have taken so far." "An excellent course, should be required for every student to take." "This course should be required by state law. We need knowledge about our problems before we can attempt to solve them." And, finally, this from a foreign engineering student: "This course caused me to wake up. I guess I had been asleep a long time and after many years somebody woke me up. This

course certainly changed my perspective on the environment."
The books were rated 4.0 on a 5.0 scale (4.2 for Strong, 3.7
for Nash), the guest speaker series a 4.8, the films a 4.4, and
the course over-all a 4.5. In another portion of the evaluation
form, 95 percent of the students indicated that the course either
lived up to or exceeded their expectations, and 90 percent felt
that it would be useful to them in the future. Comparing the
course to other history courses they had taken, 85 percent said
they maintained a greater interest during the course, and 80
percent said they considered the course more valuable.

Finally, 95 percent felt the course should be offered again.
I agree. I have already scheduled a revised and expanded version of the course for the Interim Term in January of 1978. In
terms of content, there will be no major changes; in terms of
mechanics, the course will count for three hours credit rather
than two and will meet three hours a day, four days a week,
throughout the month of January.

Perhaps one reason I was surprised by the high level of
interest in Nash's Environment and Americans in my survey
course was because, like so many others, I had the impression
the environmental movement had peaked out about 1970. Not so,
I now realize. And, in the words of National Audobon Society
president Elvis J. Stahr, "I think most of the talk about the decline of environmental interest and influence reflects a kind of
wishful thinking on the part of a few people who always hoped
it would decline. The fact is that our public support has never
been greater or more solid."[12] Bil Gilbert, in an excellent
recent article in Sports Illustrated, makes the same point: "As
all the available evidence indicates, the briefest and most direct
answer to the question--what has happened to the environmental
movement--is that it has become much larger in every way than
it was in 1970, supposedly the golden year of environmentalism."[13]
The movement is not so dramatically visible as it was in the
days of Earth Day demonstrations, of course, but it is more quiet,
respectable, institutionalized--and effective.

The response of the students who took my course makes it
clear that the level of interest and concern is indeed high. The
course seemed to be an effective way to capitalize on that
interest, as well as to stimulate it further. Another thing we
don't hear so much about on our campuses as we did a few years

ago is relevance. Yet, clearly, we should continue to attempt to be relevant. There is no doubt in my mind, or in the minds of my students, of the relevance of "Revising History with Ecology." Finally, I think the flexibility of this course is such that it could be adapted to a full semester format, and to any level from high school to continuing education.

As Bil Gilbert wrote in Sports Illustrated: "Environmentalists have been the most effective reformists of the past 25 years. If the reforms they are now proposing are accepted, they could well be remembered as the most successful revolutionaries since 1776."[14] Courses like the one described here should make a contribution.[15]

NOTES

[1] American Historical Association Newsletter (November, 1970), pp. 5-11. The page references given here are to the reprint of the article in Roderick Nash, ed., Environment and Americans: The Problem of Priorities (New York: Holt, Rinehart and Winston, 1972), pp. 84-89.

[2] Ibid., p. 85.

[3] Ibid., p. 86.

[4] Ibid., p. 88.

[5] Ibid., p. 89.

[6] The title was borrowed from Nash's heading for Jacobs' article.

[7] Reading, Massachusetts: Addison-Wesley Publishing Company, 1971.

[8] Second Edition, Reading Massachusetts: Addison-Wesley Publishing Company, 1976.

[9] Ibid., p. iv.

[10] "Ecology derives from the Greek root 'oikos' or house. The essential concept in ecology is the interrelation of all the

inhabitants of the house called earth. An ecologist studies these complex dependencies, and puts the long-term survival of the entire system in the forefront of his environmental priorities."--Nash, Environment and Americans, p. 5.

[11] Thank you, Garrick Bailey, William A. Settle, Jr., Roy Savoian, Jerome D. McCoy, Steven J. Bellovich, Francis S. Manning, Rick Groshong, and Paul Buck.

[12] Bil Gilbert, "My Country, 'Tis of Thee," Sports Illustrated, December 20-27, 1976, p. 76.

[13] Ibid., p. 77.

[14] Ibid., p. 81.

[15] The reader should be made aware of articles written by the two major names in the field of environmental history in which they share their experiences: Roderick Nash, "American Environmental History: A New Teaching Frontier," Pacific Historical Review, XLI (August, 1972), pp. 362-372; and Douglas H. Strong, "Teaching American Environmental History," The Social Studies, LXV (October, 1974), pp. 196-200.

Finally, I wish to thank the National Endowment for the Humanities for giving me the opportunity to study the "History of the American West: The New Humanistic Interpretations" in a summer seminar at the University of California at Davis under W. Turrentine Jackson in 1976; my special topic in the seminar was "Revising History with Ecology." I also thank all the members of the seminar for the contributions they made to my thinking in this area.

BEFORE TEAPOT DOME:
SENATOR ALBERT B. FALL AND CONSERVATION

"I hope . . . that before many years . . . have rolled around the Congress of the United States will abolish the Department of the Interior.... "[1]

Rather strange, if not downright farcical, that a person who felt that way should become Secretary of the Interior! But the statement is from a May 15, 1912, Senate speech by Albert B. Fall, Republican of New Mexico, who became President Warren G. Harding's Secretary of the Interior in 1921.

Fall's political career in New Mexico has been covered rather extensively; his controversial years as Secretary of the Interior, especially the Teapot Dome Scandal, have also received considerable attention; his tenure in the U.S. Senate, however, in the years between those two better-known portions of his life, have been largely ignored. This is unfortunate, for, among other things, a perusal of his stance in relation to conservation while a senator should help to shed light on his years in Interior.

Not that conservation was Fall's major concern in the Senate. Foreign policy held that place, especially Mexican relations, an area in which he was a leading critic of President Woodrow Wilson, and World War I, during which he was an ardent supporter of our war policies only to switch to strong opposition to Wilson on the Treaty of Versailles.[2] But Fall did have much to say on conservation in the Senate and, not surprisingly, he was consistently and vehemently anti-conservationist.

Gifford Pinchot, central, along with President Theodore Roosevelt, to the Progressive conservation movement of the early twentieth century, once defined conservation as "the foresighted utilization, preservation, and/or renewal of forests, waters, lands, and minerals, for the greatest good of the greatest number for the longest time."[3] Fall never bothered to define conservation, but on May 15, 1912, he gave in the Senate a description of it that hardly fits that definition:

The conservation of the natural resources of New
Mexico means a restriction upon the individual;
means that he must not acquire a homestead in the
most habitable portion of the State; and means that
upon such forest reserves and Indian reserves
the gentle bear, the mountain lion, and the timber
wolf are conserved, so that they may attack his
herds, his cattle, and his sheep. That is conservation in New Mexico. [4]

After the 1910 struggle between Pinchot as head of the Forest
Service and President William Howard Taft's Secretary of the
Interior, Richard A. Ballinger, the conservation movement, in
the words of David Cushman Coyle, "went on developing in relative quiet for nearly twenty-five years until its next outburst
of expansion after 1933."[5] During this period of "relative quiet,"
there was at least one person who was not quiet at all: Albert
B. Fall. Whenever he could find time between his tirades on
foreign affairs, he delivered tirades against conservation.

Many of Fall's comments centered around two specific
resources, forests and water. On May 14, 1912, he spoke out
against the forest reserve system, suggesting that the western
states got out of it only about one-fourth what they put into it.

The following day, he made a speech which occupied the
greater part of nine pages of the Congressional Record. It was
a diatribe against "forest reserves and reservations of public
lands." He had much praise for the old Spanish system which
had been established in New Mexico of making grants to individual settlers--not speculators, but settlers. This had been, he
said, "the most beneficient system of government ever established on this continent."[6] Then the United States government
came in and took over, and there were now forest reserves and
Indian reservations everywhere. What he was asking for was
that the forest reserves in New Mexico be turned over to that
state to administer, and he introduced a measure which would
have done this. As one author has said, turning the forests
over to the states would mean "the abolition of most of the reserves, for most of the western states would not take care of
reserves placed in their hands."[7] Fall did not see it this way.
If the reserves had to exist at all, he said, they could be ad-
ministered much more efficiently at the state level. This way,

he said, perhaps significantly, they would at least be put to use.

> I say to you . . . Senators, that better it were for
> New Mexico if every acre of this 10,000,000 acres
> of land in New Mexico had been stolen by some
> "malefactor of great wealth" than that they should
> remain in the condition in which they are at the
> present time, simply as a source of revenue for
> a lot of little clerks from a bureau in Washington. [8]

These "little clerks," he said, knew absolutely nothing about
the situation. He attributed the fact that the state of Texas was
so prosperous and its people so happy, to the fact that she owned
her own land.

In the area of water resources, Fall's thinking went through
an interesting change. From arguing at one point that it was un-
constitutional that New Mexico and Arizona had been forced to
reliquish control of their waters to the federal government
when they came into the Union, he made the transition to holding
that the federal government did have the right to take control
from the people of the states, but only on the condition that it
also assume the burden of profitably developing those waters for
the good of the people. [9] Still, three years after he announced
that change of heart, he was capable of lashing out at a bill
calling for a federally-controlled water power development
program:

> I believe that this legislation is the most
> serious attack that has ever been made upon the
> principles upon which this Government was
> founded . . . . Either we continue along the line
> of the policy adopted in 1846 with reference to the
> disposition of our public lands and natural resources
> in the West, or we make an entire and radical
> change. That change means that we strike the most
> vital blow at the State-rights doctrine that has ever
> been struck in this country. [10]

If Fall had a great deal to say about specific issues of
conservation, he had even more to say about the idea of conservation in general. Fall's speeches, on this subject as on any
other, were not notable for their organization--he would often

cover several different aspects of conservation in a single speech. Therefore, about as logical a way as any to deal with his general remarks on conservation is to do so chronologically.

Speaking on February 11, 1914, against the general policy of withdrawing lands, he said:

It is going to result in this, in so far as we are concerned, that I shall be compelled, I think, within the course of a year or two at any rate, to ask that New Mexico be created a national park. If the lands of New Mexico are to be taken from the settlers; if they are to be reserved by Executive order or by order of the Secretary of the Interior; if that country which remains undeveloped is to be fenced in by the Government so that it can not be used for local taxation for the support of municipal governments and for, the support of the State government, why, then, Mr. President, we shall either be compelled to ask to be included within an Indian reservation or a national park or be created into a national monument.[11]

At this point, the Senate and the galleries broke into laughter. Fall continued:

If this policy is continued we shall not be able to support ourselves, and if the Government is going to take our property . . . then necessarily the Government must assume the responsibility and we shall have to be included in the appropriations of the Interior Department hereafter so that the salaries of our State officials and those of our county officials may be paid.[12]

On January 8, 1916, Fall centered his attack on the 640-acre homestead law. He pronounced the reclamation policy of the United States an "absolute failure." A great public domain still existed in the West, he pointed out, but the greater part of it was good only for grazing purposes. A good plan could and should be worked out for settling this land with stock homesteaders, he felt, but:

> When you undertake to limit them in ownership
> to 640 acres of that dry, arid, grazing land,
> you place upon one who is so unfortunate as to
> secure the title a liability and not an asset.
> It is impossible upon 640 acres for any family
> or any man to make a living where it requires
> from 30 to 60 acres per cow for grazing.[13]

One month after this speech, Fall made one which was much more bitter in tone. He complained that when the people of the West asked to be unhampered in the handling of their resources in a way prosperous to themselves, and at the same time costing the federal government nothing, someone always objected.

> Some one in the United States seems to think the
> people of the West are anxious to take from
> the people of this country a magnificent domain
> . . . for the purpose of conferring it upon a few
> bloated bondholders or a few soulless corpora-
> tions.[14]

All the Westerners wanted, he said, was to be treated as full American citizens, as the citizens of the older eastern states had been treated, but:

> A poor homesteader applies for 160 acres upon
> the public domain in the State of New Mexico.
> He at once becomes an object of suspicion. Every
> little sixty-dollar clerk who has been sent out from
> Washington as an inspector of public lands . . .
> makes it his business to watch this homesteader,
> because the moment the application is filed appar-
> ently the suspicion is aroused in the minds of
> some of the gentlemen who are in control of
> . . . the Department of the Interior--that a thief
> is attempting to steal . . . 160 acres. Why, sir,
> they seem to think . . . that when a man secures
> 160 acres of land he takes it away with him some-
> where. Why, sir, the land remains there. It can
> not be carried away. It is there yet. It is
> paying taxes to the local government.[15]

He concluded that the government "should invite the people of the United States to acquire in private ownership the remaining public lands instead of throwing obstacles around the acquisition of these lands and their settlement."[16]

A year later, on February 2, 1917, Fall was praising Thomas Hart Benton for standing up for the rights of the West and accusing those who were in favor of more and more conservation measures of wanting to turn the United States into a "state socialistic government." They wanted to put the government "in competition with every line of business in the United States." He said that actually he favored conservation and that, indeed, there were no better conservationists in the country than the people of the West. That was why they opposed the administration of such programs as the forest reserves from Washington. It was just that the people of the West and the people of the East differed in their interpretations of just exactly what conservation consisted of. He concluded by saying:

> If the United States proposes to adopt the policy of reservation and of restraining and restricting population, if they prefer the sagebrush and cactus to the man, if they no longer want to build up homes where little children can live and be educated, then, for God's sake, let those of us who have been trying to build up the West know it as soon as possible, that we may in some way help our people to adapt themselves to the new condition of affairs.[17]

But there is no need to go on like this at great length--even though Fall did. Instead, we should attempt to answer three important questions: What motivated Fall in his anti-conservationism? What impact did he have? And, finally, what is significant about his role, what evaluation should be made of his thoughts and actions in relations to the environment?

Fall once answered the question of motivation himself by giving three specific reasons for his anti-conservationism. First, he insisted, it was the people's own resources which were being held back, their means of livelihood. Second was patriotism, which Fall equated in this instance with the desire of the country "to progress, to go forward." And finally, ambition, the desire to make money, to build, to accomplish something.[18]

Even if we take Fall's word for his motivation, there is need to place it in broader context. Essentially, that context is the American frontier. Fall was born in Kentucky in 1861 into a poverty-stricken family of Scottish ancestry, was largely self-educated, and by twenty was a reasonably successful frontier lawyer. At that age, apparently for reasons of health, he moved to the Red River country of Texas, then got involved briefly in mining ventures in Mexico, and finally settled in New Mexico, where he was a prospector in Grant County before settling down to a law and real estate career in Las Cruces. He was also soon involved in the rough-and-tumble frontier politics of territorial New Mexico.

The point is this: Fall was the product, his attitudes toward the environment were the product, of his time, his place, his life experiences. As his biographer, David H. Stratton, has stated:

> Until the Teapot Dome affair tainted his reputation, the most marked impression Albert B. Fall had left on the public mind during the years of his national public service was that of an epitomized westerner . . . in his attitude toward conservation of the natural resources Fall clearly reflected a common frontier attitude . . . he had been utilizing the natural resources in the Southwest and in Mexico as a prospector, practical miner, mining investor, farmer, and rancher for almost forty years. His belief in the unrestrained disposition of the public lands was as typically Western as his black Stetson and his love of good horse flesh. He was a remnant of an extravagant age, the nineteenth century, when the natural resources had been unlimited and open for unrestricted exploitation. Fall believed that the land, timber, and minerals of the western states should be used for the immediate development of that section, just as they had been in the older states.[19]

As Wilbur Jacobs has written, "When the sky was darkened

by thousands of pigeons, the normal, expected reaction was to kill them off wastefully."[20] Or, as Roderick Nash has written, "When the forest seemed limitless, cut-out-and-get-out was an appropriate response."[21] Fall himself, of course, was far more succinct--and blunt. He referred to the people of the East as those "who have had the pie that they were entitled to, who have eaten it, and now want to eat ours."[22]

On the question of the impact of Fall's anti-conservationism on the environmental movement, there is no need to say much, because there was not much impact. As Donald C. Swain's important work, Federal Conservation Policy, 1921-1933, has made clear, it is wrong to assume, as many have, that that period was an "unimportant interlude" in the conservation movement:

> The national conservation program, far from
> deteriorating, made solid gains during the 1920's
> . . . federal resource agencies formulated im-
> portant new conservation policies and expanded
> many of the existing resource programs . . .
> before the end of President Hoover's term of office,
> Congress and the federal conservation bureaus work-
> ing together had anticipated many facets of New
> Deal resource policy, and had laid the groundwork
> for most of the well-publicized conservation
> achievements of the 1930's.[23]

Thus, one is tempted to say fortunately, Fall was going against the grain of the Progressive conservation movement of his Senate years and of this stabilizing period after he left the Senate to become Secretary of the Interior.

Finally, how should we assess Fall's Senate career in relation to conservation?

Certainly, it should not be surprising to anyone even slightly familiar with Fall's conservation record in the Senate that he did what he did after he became Secretary of the Interior. On the Teapot Dome scandal specifically, Stratton insists, probably correctly, that "Fall went to prison for accepting a bribe, but it must be said in his behalf that with his belief in the unrestrain- ed and immediate disposition of the natural resources, and for

100

this reason alone, he no doubt would have turned over the reserves to [Harry F.] Sinclair and [Edward L.] Doheny, or to
some other representatives of private enterprise. "[24] Swain not
only agrees with this, but makes the related point that, considering Fall's close relationship with Doheny, he would undoubtedly
have received the money regardless of the oil reserve lease. [25]

Already we have noted that Fall's nineteenth-century American frontier climate of opinion should be taken into account. But
explaining something is hardly the same thing as justifying it.
There were people who were the product of the same climate
of opinion who had the foresight to be concerned about the de-
pletion of our natural resources.

Roderick Nash is considered by most the preeminent scholar in the field of American environmental history. He wisely
warns against some "pitfalls" in the field, one of which is
approaching it with "a manichean orientation, " of falling into
"the rhetoric of moralism--the 'good guys' versus the 'bad
guys. ' "[26] So no useful purpose is served by mounting an
ecological soap box to point the accusatory finger at Albert B.
Fall as one of the "bad guys" of American history. Indeed, a
challenge central to all historians of all subjects is to avoid
judging by the standards of their own day without showing adequate awareness of historical context.

Yet, ultimately, Fall's anti-convservationism must be con-
demned--for today. Attitudes and practices once understandable, perhaps even appropriate, in a frontier society of apparently abundant resources are no longer appropriate, or even
justifiable, in a frontierless society with clearly finite resources.

NOTES

[1] U.S. , Congress, Senate, 62nd Cong. , 2nd sess. , May
15, 1912, Congressional Record 48: 6495.

[2] Fall's role in these two aspects of foreign policy has been
discussed by the author in two articles: Davis D. Joyce,
"Senator Albert B. Fall and United States Relations with Mexico, 1912-1921, " International Review of History and Political

Science VI (August 1969): 53-76; and Davis D. Joyce, "Senator Albert B. Fall and the Treaty of Versailles," Proceedings of the Oklahoma Academy of Science 53 (1973): 136-144.

[3] Gifford Pinchot, Breaking New Ground (New York: Harcourt, Brace and Company, 1947), p. 505.

[4] U.S., Congress, Senate, 62nd Cong., 2nd sess., May 15, 1912, Congressional Record 48: 6491.

[5] David Cushman Coyle, Conservation: An American Story of Conflict and Accomplishment (New Brunswick, New Jersey: Rutgers University Press, 1957), p. 87.

[6] U.S., Congress, Senate, 62nd Cong., 2nd sess., May 14 and 15, 1912, Congressional Record 48: 6391-6394 and 6490.

[7] John Ise, The United States Forest Policy (New Haven: Yale University Press, 1920), p. 298.

[8] U.S., Congress, Senate, 62nd Cong., 2nd sess., May 15, 1912, Congressional Record 48: 6491.

[9] U.S., Congress, Senate, 63rd Cong., 2nd sess., September 12, 1914, Congressional Record 51: 15036-15039.

[10] U.S., Congress, Senate, 64th Cong., 2nd sess., February 1, 1917, Congressional Record 54: 2398.

[11] U.S., Congress, Senate, 63rd Cong., 2nd sess., February 11, 1914, Congressional Record 51: 3318.

[12] Ibid.

[13] U.S., Congress, Senate, 64th Cong., 1st sess., January 8, 1916, Congressional Record 53: 711.

[14] U.S., Congress, Senate, 64th Cong., 1st sess., February 7, 1916, Congressional Record 53: 2209.

[15] Ibid.

[16] Ibid.

[17] U.S., Congress, Senate, 64th Cong., 2nd sess., February 2, 1917, Congressional Record 54: 2472.

[18] U.S., Congress, Senate, 66th Cong., 1st sess., August 25, 1919, Congressional Record 58: 4284.

[19] David H. Stratton, ed., The Memoirs of Albert B. Fall (El Paso: Texas Western Press, 1966), pp. 5-7.

[20] Wilbur R. Jacobs, "Revising History with Ecology," in Roderick Nash, ed., Environment and Americans: The Problem of Priorities (New York: Holt, Rinehart and Winston, 1972), p. 88.

[21] Roderick Nash, ed., The American Environment: Readings in the History of Conservation, 2nd ed. (Reading, Massachusetts: Addison-Wesley Publishing Company, 1976), p. xiii.

[22] U.S., Congress, Senate, 64th Cong., 2nd sess., February 1, 1917, Congressional Record 54: 2398.

[23] Donald C. Swain, Federal Conservation Policy, 1921-1933 (Berkeley: University of California Press, 1963), p. 6. Interestingly, Swain makes the point that even the Teapot Dome Scandal," in the long run, helped to promote conservation thinking" (p. 68).

[24] Stratton, p. 8.

[25] Swain, p. 68.

[26] Nash, The American Environment, p. xiii.

ABOUT THE AUTHOR

Davis D. Joyce holds the B.S. from Eastern New Mexico University, the M.A. from New Mexico State University, and the Ph.D. from the University of Oklahoma. He is an Associate Professor of History at the University of Tulsa, in Tulsa, Oklahoma. Professor Joyce's first book was Edward Channing and The Great Work (1974); his revision of the Michael Kraus classic in American historiography, The Writing of American History, is forthcoming from the University of Oklahoma Press; he has begun work on a book on frontier historiography. He has also published articles and book reviews in such journals as The History Teacher, The Journal of Southern History, the Canadian Journal of History, Teaching History, Journal of the West, Journal of American Studies, Journal of the Early Republic, and Social Science.